HINDUISM

SPIRITUALITY FOR
LEADERSHIP & SUCCESS

Ultimate Spiritual Lessons,
based on the PowerTalks and MysticTalks of

PRANAY

Published 2025

FiNGERPRINT!
Prakash Books

 Fingerprint Publishing
 @FingerprintP
 @fingerprintpublishingbooks
www.fingerprintpublishing.com

ISBN: 978 93 9039 198 1

Preface

Hindu mysticism and spirituality offer some of the most powerful leadership and success lessons, which are both practical and profound. These lessons are especially important during tough times and challenging situations. This book condenses Hinduism's spirituality-based lessons in an easy-to-read yet insightful format.

The book is meant to appeal to all those pursuing success and excellence in life, particularly those who are seeking a roadmap on their personal leadership journeys. The core principles within this book apply to all: those wanting advanced insight on the subject of leadership, as well as those seeking higher achievement, true success, and fulfilment within life and their field of work.

The beauty of Hindu philosophical and mystical ideas is that though some of them are five thousand years old, they seem timeless, advanced, and relevant even today. And perhaps more so in the future. For they are based on essential values and deep insights into human nature and consciousness.

India's broad-minded ancient seers (sages/*rishis*) always sought to teach the most profound lessons through mythology, culturally adapted parables, as well as practical yet deep examples which could be positively utilized. That is why they were an integral part of the system in kingdoms and for all walks of life. Even a youthful leader like Alexander went deeply into questions of life and leadership while in India, seeking to learn and imbibe.

From Sri Ram's leadership teachings to Steve Jobs' inspiration from Hindu wisdom, we see the profound impact of India's knowledge for life and successful leadership. Today, we are witnessing a revival of Hindu mysticism worldwide, thereby making new work on the subject pertinent and timely. At a time when the world faces crisis situations of several kinds—from pandemics to conflict—Hinduism offers key wisdom for dynamic leadership and success.

This book is dedicated to the timeless seers, the rishis, *munis* and sages of India.

Pranay

Contents

C H A P T E R - 1

Bhishma and Wisdom-Led Leadership

LESSON: *Wisdom is in non-egoism. Ego creates lack of clarity and inner disturbance. It traps one's energies and generates unnecessary anxieties. Great leaders go beyond ego, functioning from the higher level of their free, vaster selves. Shake off ego and realize your highest leadership energies. This is particularly key during crisis situations. It enables one to lead with clarity, inspiration, inner harmony, real courage, and vitality.*

India's great epic, the Mahabharat, contains treasures of timeless spirituality-based lessons for leadership and true success. One episode between the eldest Pandav brother Yudhishthira and the great patriarch Bhishma stands out. After the Pandavs achieve a big military victory at

Kurukshetra, Yudhishthira is advised by Krishna to seek the counsel of Bhishma—who is mortally wounded, lying on the bed of arrows, awaiting death! Since Yudhishthira is going to take over the kingdom, he wishes to know about leadership, management, duty and dharma, responsibility, achieving well-being and prosperity for all as a leader. The lessons of Bhishma to Yudhishthira contain key Hindu wisdom.

Bhishma instructs Yudhishthira on the most crucial keys for wise and inspirational leadership. He tells Yudhishthira that leadership should be wisdom-led and not ego-led. Ego-led leadership always moves towards downfall. Bhishma says that the king is respected by his *praja* or subjects while the man of wisdom is respected by all. Therefore, the main teaching of leadership is to internalize and find one's own values and wisdom. Those who care for values, become great leaders. This is echoed in world mysticism also. For example, in Taoist mystic philosophy, Lao Tzu used to teach that the best king is one who'd rule with such egolessness, finesse, and wisdom that even the people would not know who is king! In other words, leaders who are truly great decision makers are so efficient and flowing in their work that they don't rely on ego at all. Rather, their innovativeness, commitment, passion and empowerment of people is effortless, skilful, and quietly energetic. Such leaders are true positive pacesetters.

Such leaders can solve people's problems empathetically, without their own egos coming in between.

Ego prevents human dynamism. It gives us a straight-jacketed view of ourselves and the world. Wisdom-led leadership exists where ego does not. That is one of the cornerstones of Hindu wisdom, one of its foundational principles or golden rules. The ego-led leader can never attain higher vision, integrity, foresight, and lasting good. His or her actions will be fraught with opportunism, not true value-creation. Opportunists do succeed, yes, but in a limited dimension. The true success of this precious human life that we have been given is to make full use of the *highest potential* within us: and this highest potential is that of higher un-egoistic wisdom *combined with* our value-creation at the practical level.

Through India's other great epic, the Ramayan, we get a detailed idea of what achieving excellence at the un-egoistic wisdom level and the practical level, together, mean. Via it's hero Sri Ram's persona, we can have insight into the highest values for great leadership and dynamic success. The success of Ram's character—despite all difficulties—is meant to teach us that his wise, calm, egoless, humble yet ultimately courageous leadership style always succeeds in a true and enduring manner; no further proof is needed for the wisdom-led style of leadership!

In fact, Ram personifies the highest 'Karma Yoga' or the yoga of work and dynamic action. It is a subject gone into in detail by Krishna much later in the Bhagavad Gita, yet we can see its practical application in Sri Ram's life and teachings. And the very foundation of Karma Yoga is detached and egoless action, work, and leadership! Sri Ram tells Laxman, 'Conducting all your work and actions as if you are being carried by the flow of the river, you will not get attached to these! Whatsoever actions you do outwardly, ensure that your mind remains pure.' Through this teaching Ram is presenting the very core of Karma Yoga, the main points about it being: (a) Working as if one is in an effortless flow, feeling carried by the natural energy of the Greater, and one remaining just an instrument of that greater power. (b) Not being egoistic or attached at all, rather being calm and tranquil, no matter what the situation. (c) Not letting outward action affect one's inner bliss/wisdom/real being.

Through Ram's various life incidents also, we can see the light of his higher consciousness shine through, teaching the highest life and leadership lessons. And at the same time, we also get very practical insight on his 'warrior path': as a prince, a fighter for justice, a leader who overcomes almost impossibly tough situations, and finally as a king! All through his life challenges and journeys, Sri Ram personifies the power of egoless wisdom and leadership humility combined with several spiritual values such as calmness and bravery in action as a leader. Hence, he has been considered the ideal leader for thousands of years, the ideal *maryada purshottom* or example of peerless dharma/duty/dynamism.

Ram was very thirsty for wisdom as a young man. All great people display a healthy regard and thirst for spiritual wisdom, called *mumukshu* in Hindu wisdom. It is a cornerstone for becoming a great, evolved leader. It creates insight, vision, and a deeply rooted strength within the individual. Ram questions the royal sage (*rajguru/* rishi) Vasishtha on various aspects of life and leadership, and their discussions form much of the template upon which Ram's leadership ethic of humility, combined with highest courage, is based.

Thereafter, we can see the egoless conduct of Ram when he chooses to renounce his claim on the throne and instead take exile to the forests just in order to fulfil his parental obligations. This is despite the fact that the people of his kingdom Ayodhya love him intensely, his brothers worship him almost, and all are prepared to fight for his rights! Yet he prevents that, and peacefully, calmly, *sacrifices* his interests in view of higher values. All great leaders should be prepared to do that: Steve Jobs once asked his chief designer Jonathan Ive what he had *sacrificed* for his vision. Self-sacrifice is key to gaining inner power, inner strength. That is a cornerstone of all mystical teachings. And the greatest sacrifice in the Sanatan Dharma or Hindu knowledge (as well as in Jainism and Buddhism) is the sacrifice of personal ego. The sacrifice of egoistic thinking leads to a quantum leap in the evolution of the individual's consciousness, and within his/her determination and decisiveness. It also sets a great example for others, as well as making one shine in the eyes of people. It creates true respect: the most important quality that a leader should command!

We need to understand that the *real warrior* is never egoistic. Ego will only stunt the warrior's skills, and slow down the swiftness of action. There has to be an egoless clarity within the warrior: cool, determined, steely, flowing with energy! That is the ideal of warriorhood personified not only by Sri Ram, but within the 'warrior code' of several world cultures, including the Japanese samurai 'Bushido' code. Sri Ram best exemplifies egoless warriorhood as he fights various enemies without any sense of personal enmity as such! But only out of a sense of justice. Not vindictiveness. Great leaders realize that personal vindictiveness is a waste of energy: it's always best to move in a *dharmic* or dutiful manner of unattached, egoless leadership. Such an attitude brings peace and fulfilment in the leader's own life as well as creates real social strength in society. And that is what Sri Ram does.

He does not display personal enmity or vindictiveness towards Ravan who has abducted his wife. He in fact displays egoless wisdom and calmness even in the face of the huge challenges on the way to defeating Ravan! And the biggest example of Ram's egoless wisdom is when— after Ravan is defeated and is dying—Ram tells Laxman to show Ravan real respect, and to learn from him!

In summation, *Sri Ram as a leader has commanded respect for thousands of years* because of his egoless behaviour and ability to give respect to others as well as to spiritual values. The greatest way to earn respect is in fact to give it where it is due, and that needs wisdom-led leadership instead of ego-led leadership!

East Vs. West: Leadership Styles

LESSON: The quality of the seed determines the quality of the tree that comes from it. Let your leadership decisions and thought process flow from your innermost seed of joyful consciousness: calm, optimistic, and inwardly peaceful. This generates hope, strength, and trust within people. It is the secret of charismatic leaders. The principle of acting from one's deepest self-realized consciousness, is key to Indian spirituality: it applies to the pursuit of excellence in general, helping us move towards true success and brilliance.

The Eastern world has, throughout history, placed much more of an emphasis on self-realization *(atma-gyaan)* compared to the West. This was expected to be a quality that even kings, generals, and leaders of all sorts were supposed to imbibe. It is not about strength alone, but about internalizing to a degree that the inner light of self shines through in every action that one undertakes. This leads to deeper vision, effectiveness, and energy as a leader. It also creates more harmonious, symbiotic, and unified teamwork. This holds true for *all* leadership and team situations: in the office, on the sports field, on the field of battle, or any other human pursuit.

It is not only Krishna's famous Bhagavad Gita that echoes this teaching of self-realization, but also other crucial texts: Ashtavakra Gita, Avadhut Gita, Ram Gita, Purjan Gita, Ramana Gita, Anu Gita, Uttara Gita, Uddhav Gita, and others.

India and the East are very rich in spirituality for practical living, very sure in the outlook toward all of human endeavour. Now, the differing sensibility of East and West is reflected in mythology. While much of Greek and Western mythology is steeped in legends of conquering heroes and their adventures, Eastern mythology always balances out the stories of heroes with a greater emphasis on the spiritual side of things. So the hero—who is the archetype of the 'leader'—is supposed to be a person of great balance. His or her quest is all about striving in the material sphere not due to any egoistic ambition, but rather essentially to serve the purpose of spiritual advancement. Also, in the Western world the advancement of materialism has been given a far more important place. But really, all that gives life meaning and makes it worth living must be found in our deepest sphere: to reach higher in your potentiality you must understand that the science of spirituality is extremely important. And one very valid reason for this is that it creates certain expanse as well as relaxation of vision. One is not trained all the time just to achieve a material goal, but one has an understanding of the broader implications of one's world vision. And this broadening of vision implies that one becomes a little less obsessed with results, and instead relaxes and loosens into one's own natural state. Only in this essential naturalness does one's potential truly manifest. So the right attitude to leadership is if we are able to reconcile both Eastern and Western thought.

And this balance is not only toward outer richness. It is also toward inner richness. And that is essentially what truly evolved leaders seek to manifest, not only within themselves but also within those they seek to lead. So when I am talking about East and West it is not so much about history. It is about an attitude, a certain vision toward life. In order to create a truly global vision, Western and Eastern thought must come together, and understand each other much more. Only in such synthesis does division disappear. And this division is basically not so much of anything else, but of reconciling the material and spiritual opposites of life because both have a part to play in the well-being of a person.

The West has traditionally been more power-oriented, strength-oriented, whereas the East always emphasizes that true strength came from within. So it's about the inner treasure. It's not so much about the outer position of power. It's about fulfilling ourselves—and whatever role we find ourselves in as leaders—through deep introspection (and in a way through a spiritual attitude). And this attitude is basically to be alert to the working of one's being. The orientation of the East is more towards what we can call the 'spirit' of man, instead of just the body-mind and material possessions.

But in an ultimate sense, there can be no difference between the West and the East. Because essentially this division is only one of attitude. The person in the West can very well have a very Eastern outlook, in the sense of being introverted (we must also understand the power of introverts as the foundation source of dynamic action). And a person in the Eastern world can have a very extroverted kind of a position. So ultimately, the great synthesis between introversion and extroversion is the key to successful and balanced action as a leader. It's about being both active and passive. It's about being capable of going deeply inwards as well as acting with very strong determination in the outer sphere.

Wellness and well-being in an Eastern, Indian, and Hindu context implies many things. It implies the pursuit of wealth; it implies the pursuit of spirituality; it implies the pursuit of pleasure; but it also implies the pursuit of that which is transcendent to everything. Only in such transcendence is there peace of the soul, bliss of the heart. Only of such transcendence arises a different sort of charisma in a person. It is important to understand these things, because in the Eastern world everything is said to move in cycles. So everything that happened yesterday is also relevant today and will be tomorrow. Everything follows certain cyclical patterns. So it therefore becomes important for us to understand what happened in mythology, and ancient wisdom. So that we can utilize this to the utmost.

Liberalism with regard to the material vision has always been important in the West. Liberalism with regard to religion and spirituality has always been important in the Eastern world. Even more so in India and Hinduism. In fact, so much so that Hinduism has also included the *material theory of the charvaks as a spiritual theory almost!* So there must be a balance of the material outlook and the spiritual one. This is the crux of it. And this is what a leader must seek to understand, if at all she or he is to create a truly lofty legacy. If you observe the leaders of the past two or three hundred years, you will find that those who have been able to successfully combine both these aspects of life have stood head and shoulders above others; they've actually become legends in history, leaving everybody else behind in the respect they command as leaders.

CHAPTER-3

Co-Operation:
The Key to Team Spirit

LESSON: Create a joyful and participative spirit within people by yourself being open and co-operative. Let them feel equal stakeholders in the effort, whatever it may be. This quality of empathy with others creates gratitude and energy. More importantly, it makes you feel fulfilled, happy, and productive. And that spontaneously leads to a resonance of well-being. The consciousness of the leader impacts the team's consciousness and spirit. It determines the path to success, especially during challenging situations.

'Samudra Manthan'—the churning of the ocean—is the ancient Indian story of the Devas or gods working in co-operation with their enemies the Asuras or demons to produce Amrit (the nectar of immortality). The story teaches us that in order to achieve a larger good, and to create abundance and prosperity, we have to work together with the deep spirit of co-operation, sometimes even with people we do not like! Then, great results are produced. Our abilities as leaders and team workers find better direction and strength through this principle, because synergies are better employed along with a creation of *esprit de corps* (team spirit) for the joint effort/combined effort.

We should not hesitate to co-operate with others, as that is the key to material and spiritual prosperity. It is the fundamental, key thing when it comes to teamwork, leadership and success in general. But co-operation requires that you work from your heart. That there be a certain warmth between the members of the team. They cannot just be aggressive with one another. A subtle aura of genuine good feeling is to exist. That allows the best energies of individuals to work in tandem with others' energies.

When things happen through the heart, they become infused with a magnificent joint energy. That is when work is transformed into something useful. That is when there is synchronicity between people, and deep rapport builds up within the team. The whole idea is that boundaries between people should start becoming irrelevant, no matter what our personal beliefs are.

When it comes to the team, a good leader tries for a harmonious coexistence between the team members, at least for the task at hand. That is positive leadership. So it is about cultivating both the sensitivity and the sensibility of co-operation. It so happens, however, that in teams of all kinds, the leaders are sometimes wrong in their approach. They are often divisive and anti-warmth. And that is a great shame because the real proper method of accomplishing large tasks is to make people more effective and simplified in their approach. This implies removing those things which create conflict. It is not about manipulating people, of being clever with people.

It is about the basic principle of creating a strong team spirit for the particular task or objective. The team spirit brings the spirit of victory! Even prior to the challenge, the team feels up to the task if there is spontaneous co-operation within the team. The individual members go beyond themselves and do all that is required for meeting the goals and aims.

You see, teamwork is all about creating a very vigorous team psyche. And that only happens when people are illuminated in heart and mind through the sensibility of co-operative effort. If this sensibility exists it becomes like different streams all flowing into one river, and this great river flows with tremendous force and energy into the ocean (which is its final goal). So all the streams have to come together, and flow in the same direction. Each in different ways, but for this then even a small team can be far more powerful than a stronger team.

We live in an age of great competition. But even amidst aggressive competitiveness, teamwork should be about greater internal co-operation. The mental attitude can determine the outcome of every challenge, so the inner spirit is more important than anything else. And the leader's job is to pool the energy of each member in such a manner that it is not lost. The individual energies combine into a steely resolve and determination!

Usually, in teams, a lot of energy is depleted and leaks through personal likes and dislikes. So the sum of all energies becomes less than what it could be. But in a truly effective unit, more energy is created as a group than ever could be as individuals. This needs a glue, and that glue is the co-operative attitude. The feeling that we are all interdependent on each other, to create something that is larger than us individually—this should be the joint attitude. So, leaders need to understand this very clearly in order to be really effective. Then only will they be able to create something more valuable than what previously existed.

In fact, this is the final test of a leader—the ability to bring people together to create something more valuable, else his or her contribution does not stand for much. The science of warriorhood in ancient India was not just about the individual heroism of the Kshatriya or warrior. Rather it was about pouring the warrior's individual energies totally and completely into the team effort, and thereby removing the insecurities that people felt with each other so that they could overcome the common challenge or the common enemy more easily. It is all about creating a tremendous quality of trust between people, and through this trust, anxiety about each other is destroyed. So all the clashes, all that is the negative aspect, can be destroyed through a feeling of co-operation.

This is demonstrated very amply in sports teams. You can observe good leaders in cricket or football, and you will find that this is the quality they have: to remove the negative aspects between team members.

In summation, only if the leader becomes more conscious about this aspect of deeply internalized co-operation, he or she is of real worth. There have been many leaders throughout history, but very few of them have attained such a consciousness which truly encourages such co-operation. Most people find it easier to divide and rule. But that is, spiritually, the wrong approach to work.

In life, we need to understand that the truly Dharmic quality of a leader surfaces when he or she transcends the basic requirements required of them, and moves to the more essential requirements. The first of which is creating this task-oriented focus through co-operation and trust. This is the basis. If you want to do great things as a leader, you have to create this space of co-operation as the base. It is the greatest space as far as leadership and teamwork go, because it is all about supporting and nourishing each other's existence. To such an extent, that individual fulfilment is also found, as well as the team's success. And this individual fulfilment is very important, because that is what creates organizational strength for the future. It is not enough that we ensure co-operation only for particular tasks, but it should become a quality which permeates as a key value in the organization. Then only would we be fulfilling the maximum possibility that the team and the individuals within it are really capable of!

CHAPTER-4

Adaptability and Flexibility

LESSON: Don't hold on to pain or past failures. Each moment is a fresh opportunity to adapt and evolve. This attitude is the difference between great and mediocre leaders. It is a very important lesson for overcoming challenges and tough situations.

The capacity to be supremely adaptive to one's ecosystem is the hallmark of a great person or a brilliant leader. The analogy given in Hinduism is that a person has to be as adaptable as a blade of grass when the storm comes, instead of trying to be just a big tree. The thing with trees is that they are strong but they break during storms. Whereas the grass is willing to be adaptable: in order to adjust to the situation, it moves with the direction of the wind. And therefore, in many ways it is even stronger than the big tree.

But sometimes leaders may want to look down over others, like tall trees towering over others! Hence, it is sometimes easier for them to break and fall. Rather, they should try and be like the grass—adapt themselves, be a little more flexible in their inner functioning, instead of just being seemingly tall yet brittle, breakable. Adaptability is really what being alive is, and what evolution means is a state which is always adapting, not static. It means a state where you keep on flowing and meet uncertainties. You are willing to take on various forms in order to fulfil the task and achieve your results. The problem with most leaders is that they sometimes miss the possibilities that are available to them. And this is because of the fundamental error: that they do not remain in a flowing and free state of functioning.

The opposite of adaptability is adamancy—to become hard and fixed in one's vision or one's scope of work. And that is exactly what is not needed in a very rapidly evolving world. A leader is a facilitator of the group's movement: he has to guide the movement of the group. If he himself is not willing to move with adaptability then the movement of the team itself becomes less fluid. And with this loss of fluidity in the group and the team, the movement toward achieving the results becomes restricted.

Life is a constant flux, a constant evolution. We have to keep on breaking structures and evolve according to new situations and new successes. We live in an age of immense disruption, and this age of disruption is about breaking structures every day. So the leader has to be able to adapt to this non-structural mode, and has to keep on breaking yesterday's structures (while in fact he may have to create new structures). But these structures need to be adaptable. It does not mean psychological weakness—rather it is the opposite—it is a state of spontaneity, a state where we are not afraid to move forward even though we may have made a mistake. And that is what true leadership is.

Often leaders get stuck onto ideas, techniques, or methodologies. But truly evolved leaders are very conscious of the fact that they are not to get stuck. Because that's what destroys and kills not only their own potential to rise, but also the organization's. This is important at every level—whether one is working in a business unit, in marketing, in sales, in product development, in public life, etc.—the ability to not get caught up in particular ideologies but to rather respond in a very alive manner (depending on whatever situation faces you). This is the key to adaptability.

And what does adaptability do? It allows you to bring various new and different dimensions into one cohesive whole. You are ready to invent new things; you are ready to create a freshness of energy, a freshness of thought. You move away from the traditional way of doing things. So essentially, adaptability begins with the right attitude or right state of being. Where you are non-attached to a previous way of doing things. You have the ability to move on from the past.

In Hindu mythology, the analogy used is that of the difference between a river and a lake. A lake does not have a flowing movement; therefore, it can never be as dynamic as the river. The river is one which reaches the ocean eventually. The river is the one which thereby fulfils its larger goal. Be river-like in your entire methodology and in your psycho-spiritual attitude. Then you will be able to reconcile the different dimensions and newness of circumstances that confront you at any point.

Leaders should have the capacity to move from fixed positions to dynamic positions. So, adaptability is dynamism. It means loosening yourself. It means not being hard and fixed or rigid in your opinions. Rigidity is the root of all problems in the world—whether this is religious rigidity, rigidity in the business landscape, political, or ideological rigidity. All things that are rigid must eventually fall and fail. They become very brittle in their quality. Have the quality of suppleness, because through suppleness and adaptability comes the ability to both expand and contract as the situation demands. You see, a person needs to have a rhythm—when expansion is needed, they should be able to expand, when contraction is needed, they should be able to contract.

All things in the world follow a rhythm: night follows day, summer follows spring, and so on. The ability to move from one situation to the other is wisdom. It is the way Nature has been explained in Hinduism: that it is extremely alive in its ability to change. So a leader should be able to change in such a manner, like nature does. Lose your sense of rigidity and stubbornness, and then you become free to soar as high as you want. And then you can reach even greater heights of success than you previously thought.

When it comes to relationships, this is very important—to be adaptable to all sorts of circumstances and opinions. So that we can find a certain rhythm with people, and vibrate with them at the psycho-spiritual level in a certain oneness of thought and action. The ability to integrate people together is a function of adaptability, of thought processes and impulses. So that you can utilize their energies in the best manner possible, instead of requiring them to change. It is good for a leader to have an immense ability to change his mind, so that he can bring about positive change in the entire team.

So it's a question simply of being multi-dimensional

instead of being uni-dimensional in one's attitude. Adaptability in movement, in impulse, in action, adaptability in communication: these are all key factors when it comes to great leadership. Each moment brings its new circumstances, and the good leader is able to actually react to that circumstance instead of repeating something that has been done in the past (in an almost mechanical way). There is a need to get out of our modes of obsessive thinking or mechanical thinking. Just because something worked in the past does not mean that it will work again in the future. And, in fact, that is the real and new reality, especially in the business world.

So, real strength is always in adaptability. Real strength always lies in certain openness: to unfix yourself from your own conditioning, and become more and more capable of relating to the circumstances that keep changing, as well as to people.

The interesting part is that nature has created an immense ability for us to adapt. In fact, the whole basis of the theory of evolution is the ability to adapt to our ecosystem, to our environment. This ability is essentially inbuilt in us, but strangely enough it can be seen that animals are much more adaptable than human beings. Because of the human mind, we have become less spontaneous and less fluid in our ability to fit into circumstances. Human beings tend to live from the past.

They tend to live from the point of view that they've been brought up in. But true intelligence is the ability to move on from whatever ideology we have been surrounded with, free of our conditionings. That ideology may have been a political one, a religious one, but now onwards it should not determine our attitude to work. We should not be fixed in our views, and especially a leader should not be fixed in views.

Charisma of leadership implies being able to give a real response to the situation at any moment. That is what creative leadership is. So it is basically a creative attitude, where you are less willing to follow the status quo, but instead are perceptive enough to fit into circumstances in the best possible manner. And to lead from this enhanced perception of reality. The very nature of material life is that it is without consistency. Interestingly enough, in Hindu mythology life is described as a continuous flux, a constant movement from one situation to the next. So, in that way, human wisdom has always been very much in sync with what modern science is now saying.

So a leader must be prepared not with fixed answers, but with responsiveness that comes not only from his thoughts, but from his feelings (or 'heart'). So, feelings are also involved. That is the way one can help others adapt also. There is this ongoing debate about whether super computers and artificial intelligence will eventually be able to replace man in his most crucial functions. But what scientists have not been able to address properly in this evolution of computing has been to make machines adapt with effortlessness like living beings. Human beings can adapt much better than any artificial intelligence can.

A child has a natural ability to adapt. Children are more adventurous in their outlook. They're inquisitive and more mentally flexible about new things. So it is important for us all to be, in a certain way, childlike, with a sense of wonder. And to bring one's ability to look at things in a new manner. This brings a greater depth to our lives. We must also remember that as leaders we should not keep complaining about things, because essentially it is about our own mental stagnancy. New problems cannot be met with predictable responses. So one good character trait which a leader must be armed with is to be completely adaptable.

In the old spiritual traditions, it is said that one needs to be completely dead to the past, so that one can almost take 'rebirth' into the new situation. So again, this question of being 'reborn' into new situations is at the heart of man's existential quest. Metaphorically it is called the concept of 'Resurrection'. This has been used in Christianity but it is also very reminiscent of ancient Indian Vedanta. It is basically a metaphor: for rebirth, to look at things with a new eye, to completely meet new situations head-on, with dynamism of spirit and attitude.

People are usually happy within comfort zones, when they have a fixed frame of reference. But that is what separates excellence from mediocrity when it comes to leadership. A leader does not like fixed frames. In fact, a good leader is a breaker of fixed frames, so that new solutions can emerge even to old problems. One has to be able to adapt and adjust so that one can cope with the current realities and future realities as they are. Sometimes this ability called 'consistency' often leads to miscalculations of new circumstances, because human beings give very fixed meaning to things. This is a problem in all spheres of human activity. In the realm of science in particular. Even in religion, in matters of spirituality, in arts.

All institutions are very reluctant to be adaptable; hence it is up to the individual and not the institution to bring about this adaptable dynamism. Then slowly do institutions and organizations too become adaptable. Don't expect the organization first to adapt to you. Adapt instead to the organization. A lot of people have problems in adjusting to new organizations, and hence do not rise as leaders within them. But the only way to ensure that your potentiality meets its highest fruition is to add this ability to be adaptable. This is the catalyst which will enhance your other abilities.

Wisdom always lies in being adaptable. It is called the way of water: just as water can fill any vessel and take any shape, so too is the mind of the leader. It has the ability to respond perfectly, with wisdom and grace, to the situation. Move with the winds of change. Move spontaneously. Like the grass which the storm cannot harm, simply because it adapts and moves with the storm instead of against it. So the adaptable person becomes more enriched in experience, and is not fixated with preconceived ideas. And that is how real genius is formed, that is how great things happen, how new things happen.

The attentive mind is an adaptable mind, because it knows the reality of the moment and can act with imagination and sensitivity according to the very situation that it is faced with. And that is the primary and fundamental strength that a leader must master, because responsiveness is at the heart of great leadership. Eventually there is no certainty about anything working out in the world of business or politics, for example. Things get redundant and can be replaced so fast. So in order to not become irrelevant in the future ourselves, we must have the ability to not run out of sync with the times. Be always ready for the future—that should be the ideal of a leader. To be absolutely ready for things. This also requires a certain courage, because you do not become afraid of making mistakes, you do not become afraid of learning through mistakes. So the ability to grow and learn is synonymous with the ability to adapt. You're not to be scared of future results.

The only real learning happens through adaptability. In fact, a leader must work on himself or herself in order to imbibe this very lesson. It is very important not only in Indian and Hindu spirituality but in spirituality around the world, particularly that of the Far East and the Orient.

There are several times that you find leaders unable to make quick decisions. They become very indecisive. This is the result of getting caught in the trap of past knowledge and past conditioning. They are trying to adjust to new situations but are relying on old methodologies, old ways of thinking which they bring with them, which might have worked for them in the past but no longer do now. That is the very nature of life and business—the only constant is change. So unless you meet this change with the totality of your adaptive ability, you become totally exposed and can become redundant before you know it.

The only real protection a leader can build for herself or himself is to inculcate in themselves an ability that allows them to face uncertainty, through an attitude of sensitivity to change. Real adaptability is about sensitivity to change. That is the whole basis and crux of it. You have to be sensitive to change. That's a very fundamental rule which every leader should look to in order to move more rapidly and readily with reality. To give shape to the reality you want, you have to deal with things not with a one-sided approach but with a multi-dimensional approach. This allows you to address the current situation in a manner that is non-static.

It is very interesting that in Indian mythology, especially in the Sankhya philosophy, reality is represented as interplay between *purusha* and *prakriti*. And in China the same reality is portrayed as the interaction between yin and yang. In both cases it is the interaction and rhythm between the feminine and masculine aspects of existence or reality. From a leadership point of view, we should be able to deal with broad dimensions of reality not in a one-dimensional manner but as a rhythm between such polar opposites. And in order to deal with opposites, we must have a mind that can adjust to both sides of the coin. Sometimes, in existence, prakriti is important and sometimes purusha is more dominant. And so on and so forth does the cycle continue. In a metaphorical manner, for leadership, we have to understand that it is almost like a peak and a valley—sometimes you have to ascend the peak and be on top of the mountain, and sometimes you have to come down into the valley. Both aspects are important. It's like a graph—up and down. You cannot constantly expect to remain in one mode or one mindset throughout your leadership journey. Have the ability to look at both sides of the coin. Have the ability to look with a more all-encompassing vision, and then do your leadership virtues truly become strengthened.

CHAPTER - 5

Temperament and Communication

LESSON: The simplicity of a calm temperament allows one to function freely, without blocking one's innermost energies. The quiet, tranquil yet dynamic mind is the powerful mind. It makes one relatable and well-liked, thereby leading to strong bonds and networks: a vital key for leaders. Truly great people and great leaders throughout history have had the ability to cultivate a happy temperament, leading to spontaneous well-being within oneself and within those one leads.

In the Mahabharat, Karna and Arjun are shown to be equal warriors—equal in skill and might. But because of a better temperament, Arjun ultimately emerges victorious. He also receives the grace of the greater power of Krishna. He is polite and balanced, whereas Karna is often hot-headed and rash.

We have to learn that a good temperament leads to greater success and higher achievement, and helps us develop better communication and interpersonal relationships. We should not be rash or angry in speaking out, in writing mails, and so on. Now, as a leader, what is the secret of having a good temperament? The first thing to understand is that one is to become more and more receptive to others, more open in one's ideas. The essential core of good temperament is to become available more and more to whatever is present, instead of blocking out things from yourself. Aggression is the result of mental energy that is basically blocking out other things and other people. You have to improve your inner conditioning, your mental attitude.

There is one very important reason why Lord Krishna chose Arjun to be the recipient of the Bhagavad Gita teachings. It is because Arjun was more open in his attitude, more receptive, than any other warrior on the field, besides being Krishna's friend. He was also a very involved and compassionate person.

It is said in the old texts that true victory can only be over your own self, not over others. He is the true warrior who can achieve victory upon his own being. It is a victory of consciousness, and that leads to dealing with others with a better sense of communication. It is simply called looking at your 'original face', seeing who you truly are. What is really important is that you are so centred in your own being, that your temperament remains in a smooth state of functioning. That it does not get caught up in situations where it can be exploited.

The problem with Karna is that he often becomes so angry, that he loses his own power. And that is eventually how he dies. So a good temperament makes one really powerful, and a bad temperament simply weakens one. This is a very essential learning for a leader to absorb. It makes the entire difference between going higher in stature, or falling.

You would notice that most leaders who have displayed a good temperament have the ability to fall into tune with the wavelength of others. They empathize with others, and that is what is truly needed for a leader. To ensure a smoother communication, that allows them to convey with power and conviction whatever it is that they need to convey. On the other hand, you'll always find that leaders of a bad temperament simply believe only in their own power, and not in the power of others. And that is the way they begin to fall. They start thinking that they are really all-powerful. They don't realize that this power has been invested in them through not just their own work, but also due to some favourable circumstances. The moment the ego tries to prove that it is more powerful than the other, it falls into the habit of bad temperament. And that is the easiest habit to fall into.

Anger is a very obvious display of the ego. So the problem is not anger itself, nor bad temperament itself. But it's got to do with the root of your being. That is the root we have to work on. Be more affirmative in your reactions to others, be more spontaneous and fresh. One should be in a constant search, a constant transcendence, of one's ego. We need to realize that anger is a very poor substitute—and ego is a very poor substitute—for authenticity of being.

The egoless state brings such joy and mental acceleration that it liberates you, and in this very liberation arises great energy to do infinitely more than that we have done so far in our lives. To be of such temperament simply means that you become more aware of your own being— it's full of light, it's full of bliss, it's full of consciousness. But in states of anger, we are missing out on this sense of being, this sense of laughter, this sense of joy. In the old Hindu texts it is said that God is not himself very serious, because if he was serious how could he have created such a wonderful world? It is such an intriguing cosmos, full of beauty and wondrous things!

The quality of creativity cannot exist along with rash temperament. Yes, it is true that great artists and inventors often have a bad temperament. But several of them use anger as a device to get things done, and it is not necessarily a reflection of who they are. In them we see a state of creative flow and joy. So anger can be utilized in the workplace as a useful tool, but that does not mean that it takes over us in a way that we lose our sense of inner relaxation and grace. Nor that creative power that we have within us, and out of which arises the real luminosity of charismatic leadership.

CHAPTER-6

Leadership Presence

LESSON: We are part of the divine fabric and creative principle behind the cosmos. We reflect its bliss and are embodiments of it: 'Ananda Swarupa'. Looking at oneself as part of the divine universal matrix unlocks one's innate energies and charismatic presence. It allows one's inbuilt capacities to shine bright in all endeavours, including leadership roles.

One of the most powerful teachings of Hinduism is that each one of us has a divine nature within.

Our life and our work is just an opportunity to express and unfold this divine nature. And the first thing to understand is that we have to discover our real work, and not waste our lives pursuing something just to prove a point to oneself or to others. Follow your heart's real desire. That is the key to growing not only in work and as a leader, but also spiritually at the same time. It is about your own intuitive abilities. About how to act from the centre of your being in a spontaneous manner, which automatically leads to an unfolding of your highest divine nature.

There are two sides of the brain—the left and the right hemispheres. The whole idea is to function through both rationality (left brain) and intuition (right brain), to combine the feminine and masculine parts of ourselves which mysticism says exist within each individual, as we have discussed previously (in India: Prakriti-Purusha, in China: Yin-Yang). Both these natures are inherent within every being. Spiritual growth as well as material growth implies a union of both these aspects in all that we do. The whole idea is to be not just linear or rational in one's functioning, but also bring in the elements of more and more creativity into all that one does.

The creative ability in man is the reflection of the divine. Therefore, it is what brings us closer to divine nature, and all things—people or just circumstances—respond positively the closer we move to our own essential nature or divine nature. It is not just about the effort we exhibit in our work and in our leadership roles. Have the ability to accept that there are deeper and higher things that function within us, and that we are to manifest these things into all that we do, even in our work situations.

We originate from a higher source and we go back to it. The spiritual attitude is to manifest this source, the central part of our existence through all the levels of our being. That is the most significant and worthwhile thing in life. But it is essentially about being aware of your own inert, hidden treasures, your own mastery. All of us have the ability to tap into deep sources of potential within, but most of us miss doing that because of our anxieties. We have to come to the understanding which the Rishis constantly spoke about, that we are beyond just the body. We are the seers who can proceed and act in such a manner that not only do we ourselves feel the touch of the divine, but all those we come into interaction with also start feeling this. It is simply a quality of being which begins with the understanding that the ultimate source is within each thing, including ourselves.

This is the secret of the most charismatic leaders of all time, Krishna being the best example. Even though most people did not know his reality, they could not help but be moved by the tremendous power that his very presence brought about. So it is all about presence, and presence begins with an inward understanding and inward attitude. This attitude is up to oneself and flows into one's ecosystem.

Self-Belief, Self-Realization, and Internalization

LESSON: Internalization creates inner harmony. It allows you to go past limiting ideas about yourself, and see that in the mystic vision, there are no limits to who you are! This roots you in a deep confidence, self-belief, and realization of your highest capacities as a leader.

In the Mahabharat, before the battle of Kurukshetra, Yuddhisthira comes to Arjun and expresses his hopelessness about winning the battle. He tells Arjun that they cannot match the huge army of the Kauravs, and will certainly lose. Arjun tells him that where there is self-belief, there is always victory or *jaya*. Self-belief strengthens the roots of man, nourishing him from within.

In modern studies of neuroscience, it has been seen that neurochemicals such as dopamine and anandamide are produced when the mind is feeling hopeful, when it is filled with self-belief. This is a fundamental factor for success. Krishna reminds us always to be in our own self-nature and so do stories such as that of Svetaketu in the Upanishads.

The fundamental problem with human beings is that they lose hope and self-belief very quickly. We are full of it one moment, and lose it the next moment. But constancy of self-belief marks extraordinary leaders from others. There is a very interesting principle that children by and large have more hope and self-belief than elders. This is because life has not tired them, they have not become frustrated by life's disappointments. In the same manner, people are more filled with hope in the mornings than in the evenings: simply because the events of life or the events of the day take a toll on us! But a leadership role requires that we go against this kind of constant change between belief and disbelief in ourselves. Leadership requires a constancy of hope, more than anything else. To have this and to have self-belief is very important.

First of all, you should not feel that you have a grudge or complaint against the world. People lose their self-belief and sense of hope because they keep blaming the world for their problems! Such an attitude creates a great deal of hopelessness in them. It creates a defeatist mindset, because they feel everything and everyone else is to blame for their miseries.

And the second thing required to have true self-belief is that you need to have a feeling of goodwill towards others. Then only will you have enough trust and compassion towards the world. Have faith in yourself, never give up hope, and trust the world. That is the last thing you must give up.

And the third thing needed is that you are to try and experience the bliss (*ananda*) of life in every moment. You can be filled with bliss if you are not a complainer. Be a hopeful person. Most people do not know how to see the silver lining in the clouds. But a good leader has the capacity to do this, simply because he has the capacity to understand that hidden in every circumstance is a potential for some happiness, a capacity for some hope. And this sort of hope is not blind hope or blind faith, but shows up as a result of being able to see with insight into the world. The world is full of possibilities. So people who can see possibilities also have a very natural sort of self-belief.

Real self-belief is not born out of ego, but out of a respect for the value of life itself. It is a very fundamental principle born of respecting the value of life and of your being. To inculcate self-belief within ourselves is simply gratitude for being alive, for having the opportunity to live this particular life, for having this particular leadership role that we may be having at any point of time. All these factors are going to create a very strong self-belief, and this perpetuates dynamism in our entire mindset. We undergo a revolution mentally, because we can then see a way out of our problems instead of wallowing in them. And that is the fundamental hallmark of a good leader. It's very easy to see the ugly side of things, but a leader is able to see the upside—the potential upside as well as the aesthetic or intrinsic value hidden behind things and phenomena.

This capacity of insight is what is called internalization. It is the ability to reflect reality as it is, with all its wonder and glory, instead of taking a negative view of it. Now, one should also not have foolhardy hopes, so that one is not shattered or broken if circumstances do not fit with our wishes and dreams. This is the flipside of having too much hope: it should not break if things do not materialize as per our plans. So a good leader has a very balanced sense of hope: he's ready for defeat, but does not have a defeatist attitude mentally. That is the spiritual attitude of a warrior.

A true warrior as looked upon in ancient India was one ready to die a glorious death, but even in that there could be a victory, because a true warrior was to fight with less concern about the eventual outcome of the battle but with more concern about his attitude of warriorship. And that determined his ultimate spiritual victory as a fighter. This is what Arjun is trying to teach Yudhishthira when they stand on the battlefield. He teaches Yudhishthira that after every night comes a new dawn. So a leader is always preparing for a new dawn: he does not fear the night. This is essentially a spiritual mindset; it is essentially a mystical outlook on life. For it strengthens us at a very deep level.

The person filled with self-belief is willing to greet the world with his best vision, his best and highest prayer in the heart. He is willing to meet whatever the higher power sends him, with a spirit of hope. Each day, he treats all circumstances as if they are opportunities to succeed, and not possibilities to fail.

Eventually, it is a question of being able to perceive the totality of things. And the totality of things means not being one-sided in one's approach. Rather, being able to face whatever is going to come from the other side. Like a true warrior amongst men. Whatever the end, however the enemy is like, whatever one is attacked with, one is prepared for this at least mentally and spiritually. That is at the root of self-belief. And that is at the root of how we can maturely meet material circumstances.

The handling of material circumstances is only a

manifestation of this intrinsic attitude. It is our inner attitude that prepares us from within. We need not go by the opinions of others when we have our own self-belief, because we ourselves can look at the brighter side as a distinct possibility (instead of dwelling on the darkness of the night). If we keep dwelling on the darkness, we will not only let ourselves down, but also will let down those we lead. And that is the surest way to defeat and frustration in whatever we are carrying out.

The spiritual way is the way of self-belief. It is very interesting that the Abrahamic religions too discuss this in great detail. For example, Jesus always asks those he wants to heal whether they have true faith. It's almost like he's asking them if they have self-faith, faith in themselves. And Jesus tells them that it is not he who heals them, but their own faith which does. So this is what he conveys to them, in essence: it is the power of self-belief or self-faith that is the basis of divine faith, and eventually creates well-being in every aspect of life.

Life can never disappoint us if we look at it with the eyes of hope and the eyes of self-belief. Because then we will always be able to see something positive, even amongst the seemingly negative aspects. And that is exactly what the true leader has the ability to do. He is thereby also able to show others this positive side of things. And this very art of showing others the positive side of things is what might be called leadership vision, because it makes everybody move towards a common objective.

No bad situation lasts forever. A good leader understands this, and instils this thought in others. So do not look at things in black and white, but eventually try to see all the colours of the rainbow! All the colours are available to us in the spectrum of life, and seeing that, we are able to go beyond the blacks and whites of situations. We are able to enjoy the splendour of the entire rainbow: that is the way of hope, and with that level of hope develops real passion in life and work. That is how you develop an attitude towards joy, an attitude of excellence, and of creating true value.

The eyes which can see hope can also see true value within others, and within oneself. And that is how value is created through one's actions in the world. And eventually good leaders are people who create true value.

CHAPTER-8

Fearlessness

LESSON: Never limit your potential through fear. It is the greatest blockage towards having presence of mind. Letting go of fear is one of the most important leadership attributes. What will happen will happen. Assume the attitude of the warrior, going boldly yet serenely into things. As a leader, this allows you to confront the biggest challenges with grace and composure. Totality in action comes through courage or fearlessness: this is a principle that applies to all things.

In order to be influential, leaders are to be in a state of fearlessness (*abhaya*). Hindu mysticism says that at its roots, fear is an illusion which occurs because we remain focused on outer events. The moment we learn to be flexible and loose, and relax the obsessive grip of outer events upon the mind, fear resolves by itself.

The fearless leader is able to call a spade a spade, but he or she does not cling to fixed beliefs. There is a certain disconnectedness from one's past. Because only the past creates illusions of fear about the future. If one is honest, sincere, and truly in a state which is free of old fears, the new fears cannot harm one. Spirituality means having become aware that old fears cannot hold you anymore. It does not matter if there have been things in the past—from your childhood, from your years in education, from your years at work—which have somehow been unpleasant for you. These are always the seeds of future fears. If we can kill the seed itself through the act of awareness, then a great transformation comes about. We become free to move into the future in an utterly natural state. And this natural state is one of living life to a maximum, with a spirit of trust. Then nothing which happened in the past can affect you in the future. Life is a continuous flux and change, yet the mind gets stuck in old patterns and habits.

The problem is that our communication with life is coloured by our experiences in the past. The mind lags behind as far as living goes. And this often leads to a failure of courage. The spiritual attitude is simply one where we come out of the structures and patterns that we have learned.

This very stepping out creates a state of letting go of all negative emotions and feelings, including fear. Finally, that which is within your heart can be expressed fearlessly. So learn to drop the past, and you would have learned the greatest art in life. It is the essence of spiritual practice, and one of the key fundamentals upon which the ancient Dharma of the Rishis of India stands. It is as if you suddenly awakened with a new energy.

The whole theory of karma is the theory of being free of the circle of the past, and awakening into fresh dynamic action. It is to become aware that the past is finished with. And then only can one step out of the circle. It is like waking up in the morning: the beginning of a new day, getting rid of the nightmare that one may have had during the past. It is simply a question of waking up. It is a great freedom, because only through fearlessness is the naturally relaxed state of dynamized action and great leadership possible.

Only through the course correction of our inner fears do we come to the right track, and move ahead with great speed in our respective leadership roles.

CHAPTER - 9

Excellence in Teamwork: The Pandavs

LESSON: Great teams have the ability to create mutually beneficial energies. Anger is replaced by synergy, jealousy by co-operation, selfishness by sharing. This applies to leadership and teamwork in all fields. The secret is understanding that the same group energy can be converted and utilized for a common and noble cause.

The Pandavs in the Mahabharat are depicted as the ultimate team in mythology. We learn through their example that despite facing all kinds of crises together, a team can be united and stand solidly together if there is integrity of leadership and co-operation. This is what the Pandavs demonstrate.

Despite growing up under great uncertainty, after losing everything—including their kingdom—and facing various other difficult situations, the team of the Pandav brothers remains united. They persevere together. And where such teamwork exists, they're sure to triumph.

What is the spirit of good teamwork? It always begins with being aware that you are participating in something much more than the well-being of the individual members. It is about the collective. Each member has to feel the importance of the team. The significance of the team has to be bigger than everyone's individual pursuit. Yes, the individual pursuits are important, the sense of individuality is very important for there to be a rhythm within the team. But together they should feel rhythmically united and larger than they would be individually. Their energies need to integrate and create a mutual support system. And that is exactly what the Pandavs do.

Throughout history, the strongest communities have been those which give people a sense of being rooted and bonded together with a common core. Alignment to a common core is key to teamwork: whether on the battlefield, on the sports field, or even in spiritual communities. It is the sense of togetherness which is the heart of great teamwork. The whole essence is that there is to be a very strong sense of community. Yes, one is not to be dependent on it, but there is a very clear sense that together the team creates an unbeatable energy-field which can meet any circumstances with a lot of strength and power. This idea of being a community knit together is at the heart of a strong team. It is the binding glue between people. But at the same time one thing is very important: you are to remember that you are to be accommodating of others. It takes all kinds of people to actually create a strong team. Only people of similar mindsets do not necessarily bring in them the diversity needed. So there needs to be a certain diversity within the team, a sense that we allow the others to be themselves to the greatest of their ability. And that is what the Pandavs do. Each one brings their own strengths into the teamwork. Only then do their respective strengths complement each other.

So a leader is someone who is able to bring about this diversity, and thereby lays the foundation of a strong energy-field between all the members. Within the Pandav group, it is seen that Yudhishthira, despite all his shortcomings, has been able to do this. He has been able to bind them together. In each member of the team, be it Bheem, Arjun, Nakul, or Sahdev, there are different sets of skills. But together they are able to accommodate a joint energy-field, and contribute to it. And this unit is almost unbeatable. This is why they're able to take on all odds.

When it comes to the Kaurav army which is much

larger than theirs, together they lift each other out of their fears. And there's a subconscious communication, at an intuitive level, between all of them. And so it should be within all teams. Because of this intuitive level of communication even the power of the Greater—that is Sri Krishna—chooses to be with the Pandav side. The alignment among the Pandavs is very strong indeed. So it's got to do with the underlying vibe more than any other external condition, which a leader can create. It's this feeling of being able to coexist with energy and joy, instead of being divided by any sort of differences. And of course, the most powerful way to do it throughout history has been to create a common cord, a common bond—where there's a common challenge facing all members of the team. It is then that they unite together the best. They tend to come together in the best possible manner when a certain crisis hits them.

So the ability that the leader has is to create this common bond, this common cord of energy. But at the same time, a positive leader does it in a positive way. A negative leader such as Hitler does it in a negative way: he creates a common hatred and this he makes into the common core. But we must look to positive leadership as the example. And a positive leader does not seek to take these shortcuts. What he does is rather the opposite: he awakens each member's vision to all that is possible in the most positive manner, the most creative manner. And through this, he creates an atmosphere of mutual trust and respect. This respect is seen clearly in the interactions of the Pandavs with each other. Even though they can easily blame each other for the difficulties that they are passing through, and for each other's mistakes, they do not do so. In fact, they reach greater heights together without blaming their leader or each other.

So positive leaders show people that they can reach higher goals together, and thereby create circumstances for all to rise. Eventually, everybody should feel that they can win, and be winners as part of the team collective.

If we look at the Indian religions—and in fact at all world religions—we would find that the concept of brotherhood between monks and renunciates was always very strong. That is why religions could grow and take hold of the human imagination. So while the search for truth is an individual one, a sense of community enhances not only material welfare but even the sensibility of spirituality itself. For example, the Sanskrit word satsang means sitting together. So when people are sitting together and taking part in a religious activity—be it meditation, prayer, songs to the divine—there is created much more power within the energy-field of the team and the community. Through this energy-field comes about a feeling that greater things can be achieved individually, but also that even greater things can be achieved when we participate in this collective energy. The idea is to feed each other with hope, and to feed optimism to others.

A solitary worker can often become pessimistic, because there's nobody to goad them on, nobody to inspire them. It is like the old story about Hanuman and the other members of the Vanar Sena. Hanuman was not sure about his own strength and it was only when the other members of his community encouraged him is when he assumed his larger superhuman form. And through this form could accomplish for the army the task of going to Lanka and creating the situations for them to engage in and win the war against Ravan.

Strangely enough, within teams we notice that even people who might not otherwise talk to each other can open up to each other in such a manner which is surprising when a crisis faces them. And of course that depends on the quality of leadership, because eventually communication is a heart-to-heart phenomenon: no matter if we are discussing things intellectual or technical, still good communication requires a genuine openness of heart. So openness of heart is what leads to good communication skills. And this is what the leader seeks to inculcate within the team. And he or she needs to prove it by his or her own example, by being himself or herself open. By creating an attitude of warmth, and creating a quality of attention to each member of the group. This is the democratic outlook. Through this quality of attention comes about an opening up, an exchange of ideas between all members, and dynamism of team alignment and team energy.

When we talk about teamwork, some of the best examples we find are not only in so-called very civilized communities of ours, but within tribal societies. They have a very deep sense of teamwork. Which is why they have survived against all odds over the centuries, even though living in very grave crisis situations, or living in jungles, or living in places where it's very hard to survive. But this sense of a shared energy-field, and this openness and understanding towards each other, has ensured their survival to a large extent. You can look at the Masai tribe of Africa: the lion hunters. They exude a very positive team vibe even in the midst of their very difficult existence. This kind of camaraderie is not possible if there is not a deep empathy towards each other. It is not possible if there's not a strong alignment towards common survival. And the whole thing is that once an individual member of the team understands very clearly that his or her own survival is in some way aligned to the commonality to the team's survival, then spontaneously they begin to invest more and more energy into the team effort. And that again is a very important task the leader has to convince people of, in ways which are intuitive. That for each of them to survive and prosper, they must also make the team in entirety survive and prosper.

The leader needs to be a good storyteller, bringing all his experiences into creating a narrative which conveys to each member of the group that the question is not just about self-survival, but it is about the entire team's survival. This he or she must convey as being primary, emphasizing that of this will spontaneously come self-survival and individual survival. Individual prosperity is to be understood to follow from the team's prosperity, instead of vice versa.

The human brain by its nature is selfish on the one hand, but on the other hand it has also got a very deep capacity of empathy and of community living. This is simply because way back in mankind's history, man existed and survived only because of the strength of one's collective support system and community. So at a deeply collective subconscious level, we are inclined to be good team workers. We just need to relearn the skills. And the leader is one who helps people to learn this art of relating to each other, of fulfilling each other's purpose to such a degree that eventually their own purposes are also fulfilled.

Eventually, the best teams are comprised of people who can come totally and unconditionally to a collective team effort which transcends individual capacities manifold. The problem that often happens in teams is that there are too many voices of dissidence, and too many voices start taking precedence over others. Around the world, this is the main problem. This struggle of people within teams. But this struggle needs to be cut at the roots by leaders. So a leader is one who remains alert to this internal group dynamic of struggle. Human beings are inclined in any group to enter into power struggles. So a leader should know how to pay attention to this, how to steer it and replace it with joint creative energy. This is more important than individual power plays. The idea should be to send a message that people who indulge in individual power plays for its own sake, will eventually have to move out and lose their status in the eyes of others. So it is not an element of intimidation which is important. Rather it is to make people see clearly that the group comes first, and the leader should not hesitate to communicate that.

Eventually, good teamwork is to make people joyful—to bring fulfilment in every manner, by serving a common purpose. To bring out the value within each other is the goal. So that value is created in entirety. To create bliss within the team is important. It is not about putting each other down, but it's about transmitting a greater flow of energy from one to the other. This does not mean that conflict is not to be tolerated. In fact, sometimes conflict and friction often bring out the best in people. It is the concept of clash; when two things come to friction, that creates something new. It's like rubbing two stones together to create fire. In fact, the whole universe is said to come out of this principle of clash: where opposite principles come together to create something new. So a leader does not shy away from internal arguments or internal clash, but always remembers the primacy of a very alive communication as being paramount between members of the team. There must be constant communication, there must be constant dialogue, even if sometimes it is unpleasant. But eventually out of this dialogue can be born a familial feeling, a feeling that the team is some kind of a family.

And there is to be some semblance of structure within teams which resembles the family structure, where each person's deficiencies are accepted but also overcome through the joint effort. Eventually, teamwork is the greatest opportunity to relate to others, and the best workers are those who take advantage of this opportunity to relate and become more deeply networked, thereby establishing interpersonal relationships which takes strong roots. People who understand this, rise to leadership positions, because out of these situations of networking they can arise as leaders within the team. It is about being rooted deep within the network. It is not a question of creating an institution of the team, because in an institution itself comes problems. It's about creating a very organic organism of the team, one which is comprised of different parts, yet functions like one singularity—like a human body comprised of so many parts, but working in an integrated manner.

The basis of teamwork is essentially to be one of heartfelt alignment and spiritual fellow-feeling, because it's all about bringing out the best of one's heart and mind to the matter at hand, and to the team effort itself.

CHAPTER-10

Mythology: Mystical and Material Meanings

LESSON: The core lesson of mythology is to bring into sharp focus two leadership styles: the destructive and the creative. Intelligent leaders learn how good outcomes come through the second leadership approach. Mythology is ultimately a reminder of the most important things concerning human consciousness; we would do well to imbibe its lessons. It teaches us that changing our consciousness is the first step towards greatness.

It is very important to understand that Indian mythology has also found resonance in other world mythologies. For example, the story of Krishna resonates deeply with the story of Christ. Kans is almost represented as King Herod is in Christianity. The story of birth of both

Krishna and Christ is about overthrowing the material king and being the 'spiritual king'. So this is a thread in both stories, and there are many more similarities. But at the end of the day the whole idea is to convey that it is always the spiritual element of life which will win over and defeat the purely material element of life. That is the story even in the Mahabharat: the central idea being that when spirituality is combined with materialism, there is true victory. And where materialism and gross forces are predominant, then defeat is certain.

The same thing happens in the Ramayan. Ravan is a representation of material power, but before Ram—who is a combination of both material and spiritual power—he goes down, despite his own spiritual qualities. So really the focus of the vision of leadership has to be that you combine spirituality and materialism in a manner which allows you to view things in a much less narrow way and instead in a broad manner.

The function of mythology is to provide a very clear insight into some universal truths regarding how life is to be lived and work is to be accomplished. But if we go on creating interpretations of mythology we would find a lot of wrong interpretation happening. In fact, this is what is happening in the world today. However, the fundamental takeaway of Indian mythology is basically that the entire existence is to be looked at as being divine. Agni, Indra,

Vayu, and other gods are manifestations of nature—of fire, rain, wind, and all that nature is about. So essentially the whole idea of mythology—and the main insight in Indian mythology—is to look at things with a vision of it being part of a common divinity. This vision transforms the way of looking at the world and our own beings.

So it's fundamentally a way of looking at the world. If you look at things with an eye that sees this fundamental field of sacredness of holiness running through everything, you spontaneously become free of material and mental anxieties or stresses. Simply because now your vision has been broadened, and you are able to see things with a vision that dispels the worry.

Mythology is essentially a reflection of humanity's collective consciousness. Therefore, it has much timeless meaning for us. And that timeless meaning can be understood to be this: the deeper we go into spiritual understanding, the greater heights we can rise to in the material sphere. And this is very important for a leader to understand. In fact, it contains a very important lesson of mythology. That here on earth we can create heaven, we can create paradise, only if we have the vision to do so. And the vision to do so comes with seeing things in both a spiritual and a practical sense. Also, we have to understand that people are attracted to those with the spiritual vision. So in that sense a leader who can exhibit deep insights in his life and work automatically becomes very charismatic for others to follow. The person of insightful wisdom is always respected, and spontaneously rises to greater and greater leadership positions. Mythology is an attempt to explain the larger dimensions of reality through things that we can relate to.

The Mahabharat has profound and sublime truths, but within the realm or field of human action subjects— such as battle and warfare, leadership in politics and in material wealth, and so on. The interesting part about Hindu mythology is that it has consistently voiced things over thousands of years which are now resonating with science and modern psychology. And this part of modern psychology is very important from the leadership angle, because essentially leadership is all about psychology. If psychologically we can become sound, spontaneously our leadership abilities are magnified manifold. And we also experience self-fulfilment. So at the psychological level, to be in a state which is free of stress, a leader must emphasize not only knowledge and skills, but more than that. And that element is what we might call the 'spirit' of man. That element is what makes us exhibit our greater qualities.

It is all about moving to the highest consciousness that we can move to, and acting and thinking out of this highest consciousness. Now, it is very interesting that in the Puranas it is mentioned very clearly, and in a metaphorical manner, that even the gods can feel jealous of the heights of consciousness that man can reach to! Even the gods are envious of the capabilities of man. In fact, man is said to be an infinite energy, and every time a person attains a very high consciousness, not only do people on earth notice, but even beings in different spheres—the different celestial spheres, do so. This can be taken to metaphorically mean that there is no end to the quest for consciousness. We can raise our consciousness, and thereby raise the standard of our leadership—of teamwork, of co-operation—to create something of value. Then only will we be able to justify the potential of our *chitta* or consciousness that has been inbuilt into us as a species.

The evolution of spirituality—as well as the evolution of great leadership—is an evolution of consciousness. Mythological symbolism is simply a means to awaken us to the importance of both consciousness and materialism, together. All the spiritual traditions of India have culminated in trying to teach just the value of evolving as human beings. And through such evolution, to bring about greater contentment and fulfilment in the material sphere—in our relationship to others, as well as psychologically within ourselves. In fact, that is the entire message.

It is said that the spiritual lotus blooms within man as the *sahasrara* chakra if we can take our psycho-spiritual evolution to the highest degree. It is symbolical, simply meaning to say that all we want to bring to flower and fruition is possible if we look at things being essentially part of a broader reality. This is also the secret of the avatars such as Ram and Krishna—they come to the earth as human beings, but demonstrate through their thoughts and lives that divine ability for both material and spiritual evolution can coexist in the human form and shape. That is why *they* are such great examples for life and leadership.

CHAPTER-11

The Power of Integrity-Based Leadership

LESSON: Integrity and ethics create inner strength. They nourish a leader's power of internal energy. Through integrity, a leader's decisions acquire the ability to bring meaningful and transformative change: the mark of truly successful people. Moreover, integrity and ethics allow one to lead a quality-filled life: fulfilled within, while creating value in the material world through more authentic creative energy.

The question of integrity (*satyanishtha*) is very crucial to life and leadership brilliance, because it actually demonstrates that one practises what one preaches.

A leader of integrity is really one who does not bow down to any kind of pressure, but follows his own sense of right. In Hinduism, such a leader is considered to be the highest leader of men because he develops an intuition—a sense of having a unique and intuitively trustworthy relationship with all the members of his team. And this kind of integrity-based leadership is really at the heart of inspiring true confidence and support in people, so that the overall goals are met.

That which is called 'leadership effectiveness' is an outcome of such integrity. And integrity implies that no matter if the decision is unpopular or not, one goes ahead with it. And one functions in a manner that eventually one is looked at as a positive role model. Because it is by example that one is leading, and not just by what is convenient.

At the heart of all spiritual thought is this idea—that a leader is one who unifies people across boundaries of gender, age, lifestyle, race, and so on. That is what a leader of integrity stands for. That is what is meant by integrity-based leadership. Now, it is very contradictory to the Machiavellian sense of leadership, where you are very ruthless and are manipulating others. That is one style of leadership, but eventually if you look at it from a humanistic perspective leadership is about actually being a force of good within the world. The way of Machiavelli is not considered to be very uplifting or creative. In fact, it stifles creativity, and the leadership of the future must be exceptionally creative. Hence the question of integrity is even more important than ever before.

What are the primary things in order to become a leader who is regarded as one with creative integrity? First is to allow greater participation in decision-making. So you are participative in nature. That is what allows people to bring the best of their personality traits onto the table. It's about enhancing people's personal power. And in this manner, one not only allows others to demonstrate their own integrity and charisma, but also consolidates one's own position as a benevolent leader. She or he is looked at as one who does not only believe that they exert sole control over decisions, and control resources, but that they believe in the success of everybody around the table. This readiness and willingness to allow participation of all—or at least the key stakeholders—leads to a great deal of self-awareness within the participants, and part of that self-awareness would involve a renewed respect for the person who has given them the responsibility. It makes people feel socially significant within the lead decision-making group. You also raise your own personal profile socially through this style of leadership. You become more charismatic socially, because it shows that you're capable of multi-way communication. And that is the way to success for a leader in today's business ecosystem, societal ecosystem, or organizational ecosystem of any kind.

The second thing to remember in order to achieve full power as a leader of integrity is to invest more and more passion and love into your work. Eventually, the only way to accomplish great tasks is to truly love what you do. And more often than not, this is simply a question of choice. A person who works out of integrity is also acting out of a deep love for his work. And this leads to an enhanced vision of the organizational goals. This also demonstrates that one is willing to put one's heart and mind fully into the task, and sets a good example for others. Work ethic is determined largely by the love we have for work, and that is all part of the integrity we seek to bring to the tasks we do. It reflects a real willingness to lead, a real willingness to resolve conflicts and crises.

The third aspect of the leader of integrity is that they are never afraid to go against the image which people have of them. They are willing to discard what has been done in the past, and are not interested in reinforcing people's image of them. So they have a certain self-belief, of bringing a brimming confidence that creates a sense of real assertiveness, a sense of straightforwardness in expressing their feelings. That gives their opinions weight. This leads to a feeling that the leader is very authentic, true to himself or herself. And this in turn creates a better image of one as a leader—because eventually people always value those who are authentic. More than cognitive ability, people are looking for this ability—which is the product of integrity. It creates certainty, and this is what makes some people really attractive to others.

Finally, that which distinguishes the leader of integrity from others is an emphasis on collectivism: that society or the organization should receive more priority than anything else. In other words, concern for others, and an emphasis on building relationships with others, underlies leaders of integrity. They are able to create an environment of trust, support, warmth, friendliness, consultativeness and co-operation. All these factors lead to a deeply embedded value system, rather than competitiveness alone. Eventually, a leader of integrity is able to instil greater drive within the hearts and minds of the team, in order to achieve the best possible outcome.

CHAPTER-12
'Svabhava' and 'Svadharma'

LESSON: There are two very important principles which are at the very foundation of Hinduism: the first being that of svabhava—our inherent or essential nature. And the second being svadharma—the action which is done according to our self-nature. The basic idea is that each of us has an inherent nature and also has an inherent capacity to do certain actions which define our place in the world. Through the carrying out of such actions—our duty or dharma—if we carry out the will of the Greater or the larger aspect of existence (which exists as our svabhava), we truly succeed in what we attempt.

We are to act according to our own svabhava (essential nature) and our own svadharma (actions flowing from our essential nature). These form the fundamental basis which we must understand in order to fulfil our various life and leadership roles. These qualities awaken right determination and right energy within one, enhancing one's capacity for pure and effective action.

Essentially, these principles are what Krishna teaches Arjun in the Bhagavad Gita. The whole idea is that the principal character of Krishna in the Mahabharat is somebody who seeks to remind others of their own svabhava and svadharma. Sometimes it is Arjun, sometimes it is Yudhishtira, sometimes it is Karna. But he is always enjoining upon people not any form of worship nor any form of ritual or offering, but essentially of awakening their own capacity to function according to their self-nature.

The Dharma Shastras are the texts which enjoin upon us to do our duties. The principal thing about the Dharma Shastras is that actions done out of our svabhava and svadharma purify the individual. The Upanishads also emphasize the same thing. They are less about the ritualism and more about the underlying meaning of rituals. And that underlying meaning is the readiness to understand the essence of yourself as an individual, and to understand that this essence of yourself or Atma or spirit is a part of that greater power which underlies all existence. This is the knowledge which leads to the knowledge of the Greater, of Brahman. It is the realization of this relationship between one's inherent nature and the larger cosmic essence of reality, which truly liberates the individual and makes him one with the larger reality.

The adherence to svabhava and svadharma is the essence of the secret teaching of Vedanta, the Upanishads, and is also in sync with Buddha's teachings. This is not primarily mystical speculation, but has as its basis an essential adherence to the concept of *virya* or heroism. And that is what leadership must eventually lead to. That is the essential 'way of the warrior': fighting any battle in life, and leading effectively in any situation.

CHAPTER-13

Compassion and Well-Being

LESSON: The greatest people have the greatest compassion. Compassion is the ultimate test of mind-body-spirit evolution. It separates the extra ordinary from the extraordinary, the inspirational from the non-inspirational. Moreover, it is the highest leadership emotion, leading to passionate excellence and impactful love within all of one's actions.

The question of compassion or *karuna* is very relevant to the art of true leadership excellence. The first thing to understand is that compassion brings about a great release of energy. It is a beautiful energy which acts as a catalyst for your best qualities. It creates an overflow of good energy. If compassion becomes your authentic experience and the foundation for your actions, you will find yourself in a constantly blissful and rejoicing mode. So it is extremely relevant at the level of feelings and fundamental emotions. And that is what well-being is all about: to be in a state of feelings and emotions that helps you, rather than hinders you. Compassion implies pouring your positive energy whenever it is required, in whatever situation it is required. And that is really the foundational aspect of leadership—to have such an inexhaustible energy, that you can more easily solve problems in difficult situations.

It is the art of looking at things with the sense of wholeness, and when you look at things with the sense of wholeness, great joy comes about in your being. And the result of this joy is creativity. So in a sense it's really more precious than what happens in the external world: every leader is to remember the outer is only a result of how you are within. The inner state of being is really all that you share with the world. If it is one of good energy, you come into a good energy with the world. So it's very simple: in order to be of value, in order to be of service, the basic requirement is compassion. This is the real prayer, this is the real *sadhana* or spiritual practice. It is enough to create a state of being which energizes your actions. And that is fundamentally what every leader needs: to create a dynamic energy. So that one's actions have real value. Religion is not to be looked at as something which happens in a place of worship, because the true place of worship is within.

We are to be aware that our inner human drive creates outer abundance. A good leader is one who is non-destructive, who is creative. You may be disruptive but should not be destructive. Disruption is required in order to bring about something new. But that does not imply that you have to be hard within your heart. Rather, the way of softness is the way of real creativity; it is the way you can create something new. Like Hinduism, in the religion of Chinese Taoism there is a saying that one is to be soft and flowing like water in order to be more effective. Water is more powerful than stone because it can wear away the stones on the riverbed. To be soft and flowing like water is true compassion. To react with a sensibility that is sensitive to others, and to the environment around you. To find your uniqueness, to be respectful of the world, and out of that respect giving such inner freedom to the people you lead that they are able to break through. That they are able to do something truly innovative.

So compassion is one of the highest emotions, which leaders can use to inspire innovation and creativity.

Creating a Positive Energy-Field

LESSON: Great inner joy leads to a great energy-field. It creates hope and optimism within oneself and within those one deals with. True quality in your leadership abilities is determined by the quantum of joy and peace you generate within yourself. This spontaneously manifests positiveness and peace around you: it is the secret of leaders who are effective in action and fulfilled within their own consciousness.

Effective leadership is about creating a positive field around oneself. Human action is limited, but our ability to leave an impression is unlimited. The vibration of ourselves—our very presence—shines through the work we do, creating ripples of energy, and sends out a message whether we realize it or not. The very fact is that through everything we do, we are constantly creating a field of energy which affects people around us. Every leader must clearly understand this.

The fundamental thing to understand is that no action of ours goes waste: it either becomes an opportunity to grow, or stunts one's growth. The challenge is, how do you create a positive field of energy where growth opportunities flourish? The basic thing from a spiritual standpoint is to recognize the value of life and to respect the value of your own existence. That is key. Hindu philosophy says that within the innermost (*antartam*) parts of yourself exists the voice of the ultimate. We are to listen to this inner or *aantarik* voice, to be in touch with this hidden truth within ourselves. Hinduism is very interesting, it has very interesting perspectives. It says that while man is seeking God, God too is desperately seeking man. But the problem is man does not listen: we are being pulled by the subconscious, we are often operating out of our unconsciousness even. Operating out of true consciousness implies becoming more and more meditative. Relating to oneself at a deeper level, and thereby relating to all of existence at a deeper level. The moment this relating becomes deeper, automatically and spontaneously there arises a natural energy-field around oneself.

We must unlearn our habits of relying on outer knowledge, because it is self-knowledge which is the hallmark of a great person and a great leader. We are constantly in a state of choice, we are constantly creating our own karma, but the choice we have while creating it is this: either we think ourselves separate from existence, or we think ourselves one with it. The moment you realize your oneness with everything, a deep feeling of unity arises within you. And out of this feeling of unity comes about tremendous dynamism of being. You become luminous with the intelligence of the greater. You become noble in your vision, and through this nobility of outlook comes about an invisible energy-field that makes people more attracted to you and to what you say. You are essentially your spiritual self, and it becomes revealed more and more, manifesting as positive actions as a leader.

Man is taken to be infinite (*ananta*) in Hindu mysticism, yet we forget this infinite portion of ourselves and work only with a very small portion of our consciousness. This is the primary reason we never really feel satisfied. Because we are not creating that energy-field of infinite contentment that we have the ability to. We are functioning out of a state of anxiety, of worry, and where there is anxiety and worry we shrink into ourselves. We are not in let-go. Only in let-go do we become extensive and expansive, and out of this sense of expansiveness comes about a positive energy-field. We have narrowed the concepts of religion so much that religion itself limits us instead of being an expansive process.

The essential ancient religion of the forests—of the Rishis—was meant to release the complete energies of man and not be a limiting thing. On the other hand, most of our institutionalized religious beliefs of today limit our beings. To be in a state of let-go means you drop your beliefs, you drop your burden of self-consciousness, and move toward the space where you can live without the ego but more fully! As if everything you encounter is a blessing. This feeling—the sense of feeling blessed—is essential, as it helps you become more luminous within yourself. And feeling more luminous within yourself, the light of your being shines into the world. People forget the power of feeling blessed. If you but feel it, it will shine through you. The feeling of being blessed creates bliss. And the state of blissfulness spontaneously creates a positive energy-field. It lights up others through your presence. This is the secret of charismatic leadership. It's almost as if a light is coming from a person, as if they have an aura around them. In fact, in mythology, charismatic people have been shown to have this halo. This is nothing but a symbol to say that they're in a state of feeling blissful and blessed. This shines through in how they are with the world. It's almost as if the doors and windows of a room have been opened up after very long: suddenly you feel a sense of freedom, as if your energies are reaching outside you. The opposite way is to feel miserable in your everyday action.

There are several leaders who, due to their own lack of self-worth and lack of feeling blessed for being in the position that they are in, seem very miserable. And they are bad not just for themselves but also for the people they lead. Because all they succeed in doing is create a very negative energy-field. They fail in an ultimate sense. We must instead learn to look at ourselves this way: that we have to be constantly moving towards our own inner nature, and through this very movement towards our own nature we are also going higher and higher towards the peak of all that is good and noble within us.

The growth of our positive energy-field is the consequence of the growth of our inner consciousness. The more it grows the more we will feel capable of handling problems. In this way we become clear, transparent, and courageous enough to find new solutions to leadership problems.

The finest things in life are very subtle. So that which is valuable is also very subtle. But sometimes it becomes drowned by our fears and anxieties. Through the act of paying attention within, we open our hearts. We receive and spread more positivity in the world around us. From our innermost core must come that awakening. And in fact that is what real religion is, real spirituality is.

The goal is to be in your highest positive state. Who knows about God, who knows about ultimate truth? But the truth within you is the thing! So find the most positive within yourself, do not look for value only within the outside world or material world. Find the value within yourself and you will then feel that people feel an unknown attraction towards you. They become attracted to that light—that dynamic light which makes you luminous, which is the light of your own positive energy-field.

CHAPTER-15

Far-Sighted Leadership

LESSON: Remember that your consciousness is a treasure trove of wisdom and power, most of it hidden and unseen. It is capable of great vision. Within you is tremendous strength: never think yourself weak at the level of consciousness. Remembering this awakens your power within, making you see beyond challenges, allowing you to act effortlessly when confronted by tough situations. A visionary leader is one who has first opened the doors of his or her own consciousness, filling one's self with great courage and energy.

Far-sightedness or *durdrishti* is one of the most critical patterns that great people and excellent leaders have. It is the ability to understand long-term implications of one's ideas, actions, and strategies.

A few things are very important in order to have such far-sightedness. The first thing is that one needs a very high tolerance for disappointment, so that all sorts of hindrances that come in the way of one's aims are overcome. So first of all one has to be mentally tolerant, and ready to face frustrations of all kinds. That is the primary hallmark of a far-sighted leader. It is the vision which is important, and in order to get to that vision one is willing to go through all sorts of frustrations, no matter what.

The second quality that one needs is a great deal of emotional stability and emotional intelligence. So one's emotions have to be controlled, in order that one always acts appropriate to the situation. One is to not act harshly or irrationally. Disturbed emotions lead to instability. Emotional intelligence is nothing but understanding one's own sense of inner stability, for only then can one have empathy for others. And empathy is what leads to other people feeling emotionally enhanced in one's company. And this is eventually what one's effectiveness as a leader is dependent on. One's ability to exert influence over others is somewhat due to one's skills, knowledge, and abilities, but more importantly it needs to be tempered with emotional stability. And then only is one able to have that long-term drive within oneself. And inspire others also to put high energy into achieving common goals.

Depthful leadership is that which allows workplace harmony, and the ability to gain a competitive advantage by creating a very exciting environment so that people can enjoy work, and where they can feel that the task they are doing is really worthwhile (despite all external circumstances). Then only can one go really far and achieve real success.

The next thing that far-sighted leaders need to have to succeed is the ability to bring about positive changes, to bring about transformation, but at the same time making people believe in or having confidence in the sincerity of one's thoughts and actions. So it's a two-pronged process: one is to bring about change, but during the change it is important to have such communication that people get the message across very accurately. And one should in fact enhance the vision of meeting the common goal for all. So strategically, it is extremely important to balance out the ability for transformative change and creating confidence, so that both the direction and inspiration that are necessary for reaching the far-sighted goal are integrated—in such a manner that there is a common commitment to the group goal.

The thing for a far-sighted leader to understand is that it is important to admit one's mistakes quickly, and by doing so to go on creatively improving life. Life is a very rapid movement, hence it is very important to get on with things and to admit one's mistakes with a clear focus.

There also needs to be a basic simplicity, so that one's thinking is very clean. This cleanness of thinking is the hallmark of great leaders and great people. It takes us on to higher goals. It creates the necessary conditions for one to put in real life energy, and invest a lot of pure passion into tasks.

Lastly, the thing required for far-sightedness is that it is not the quantity that is important, but the quality of the tasks done that truly matter. Do small things, do one thing even, but do them well. Because then only will you be able to demonstrate that you have put your heart and soul into the responsibility entrusted upon you. Then only will you be able to demonstrate that you have the ability to do something wonderful no matter how small it is. It's better to have one perfect wildflower than a bouquet full of plastic flowers.

Remember that you have the power to influence things by doing whatever little you can to transform and bring about change in the world. You can create something unique with whatever it may be—never think a task is too small for you to accomplish. The first step is always the most important in a very long journey. So remember to take small steps. Then only will you be able to walk very far, and go on to that horizon which you have in sight.

The only way to invent the future is to take small steps and to keep walking. That is the hallmark of excellence. Then you will see that very soon you have approached the finish line much quicker than expected. This ability of constant attention to small tasks distinguishes innovators and true leaders from followers. It is a question of attitude: what you do doesn't have to create a revolution, but in its own way if it can make something even a little better or a little more beautiful, it is fascinating and rewarding.

The important thing is to check your negative tendencies as a leader and also check the negative tendencies of others. So that together you can move on forward for creating the far-sighted vision. To sum it up, the far-sighted leader is one who has the ability to say no to things that are not essential, and to say yes to those things that are essential.

What also differentiates a far-sighted leader from a short-sighted leader is that the far-sighted ones have an uncanny ability to not dwell on past achievements, but to move on to the next thing. And to move on with an eye on detail, because details are always important. Such leaders always know how to connect the small things, and through such interconnections they come up with something really creative. They also know how to connect people. They know that they have essentially nothing to lose and therefore are really courageous, and having such courage they have the ability to follow their own hearts. A short-sighted person has goals such as creating a certain amount of wealth and so on, whereas the far-sighted one is a quality creator—a person who measures things through the yardstick of quality—and through this yardstick comes about revolutionary change.

The whole way of looking at things is to take continuous steps forward with a lot of faith. In fact, this ability to have faith is central not only to religion but really important for leaders in the real practical world, in the material world. People who are looked up to as positive role models are those who do not persevere with the past, but who go on nonetheless despite whatever disappointments they may have had. Such people go on to be heroes for they exhibit heroic qualities. Heroes are not extraordinary beings but ordinary beings with hearts full of courage.

And most importantly, far-sighted leaders have minds which are very calm. They have the ability to observe their minds, and therefore have the ability to do things out of a deep inner intuition, out of a sense of being relaxed and a sense of having patience. This creates an expansive mind, and this can only come about through far-sighted clarity. Such leaders are not trapped by dogmatic thinking, but have a deep inner voice which is the reflection of their own intuition. They know what they really need to become, they know their organizations, they understand people, they know the kind of evolution the organization and people need to move toward. Hence they are able to push things forward with great courage, with great clarity. And in that way, they begin to change the world in their own manner. And that is true leadership, true success!

The Power of Acceptance

LESSON: Acceptance implies the maturity and patience to not be irritated by minor things. Great people and good leaders don't take negativity or criticism personally: they see the larger picture. They are attentive to details, while not being over-sensitive or over-reactive. Such an attitude creates inward power, and adds weight to one's persona. It generates a natural respect.

The Hindu concept of totality of acceptance (*sweekaar*) is at the heart of good leadership. It is basically an attitude that converts one's being into a state of joyful acceptance of enjoyment of whatever life brings. No matter if the circumstances are favourable or unfavourable, one is simply not afraid, one accepts wholeheartedly.

Through acceptance inwardly, one remains centred, notwithstanding the ups and downs of circumstances. And this is the hallmark of a great leader. To inwardly remain positive and joyful. The weather may change; circumstances may change like the weather. It may be raining outside, it could be the monsoons, it could be summer or winter or autumn, but one's inward climate does not change. It remains positive, through acceptance. One simply does not choose one thing over the other.

This acceptance of circumstances is really the concept of *poornata*, of wholeness of being. Of totality. Basically, we have to function from a heart full of gratitude. And understand that we have to function from the very core of our beings, from the very depths of ourselves, instead of being disturbed by that which is on the surface. Out of such understanding comes the vibration of dynamic action.

The problem with man is that he is constantly confused. Depending upon changing circumstances, he keeps oscillating and wavering from one mood to the other. But a good leader is a constant person. A good leader adapts to change, and this constancy is a quality of the inner. The whole idea is that we can be inwardly in such a state. And so doing, one's entire work and one's entire life becomes fulfilling. Do not be worried about that which the outer eyes are perceiving, that which your brain is processing related to outward circumstances. Be concerned with your inner eye. Be concerned with the insight which you have, which tells you that you are not to be distracted by a thousand and one happenings in the world or by the various different circumstances of the outer material world. In so doing, you do not function like people ordinarily do in ordinary life.

People keep doing their work as if it is a series of frantic tasks to be fulfilled, moving from one situation to the next, because the basic quality of inward integration is missing. But a good leader on the other hand is one who has such a crystallization of inner being, that she or he is able to reconcile the different notes of life into one central harmony.

This ability to harmonize different aspects is really what good leadership is. Circumstances change. Understand and accept that life is a wheel. In fact, it's been described by the seers of old and even the Buddhas as being a wheel. And this wheel keeps turning—so do not be worried if the wheel at one moment is not favouring you. What goes up must come down. But inwardly, you do not need to be constantly going up and down. You do not need to be dependent on this high and low.

The whole quest of the evolved person is to understand the dynamic between unhappiness and happiness. One moment, one is happy. The next moment one is unhappy. Yet you are to transcend this momentary happiness and unhappiness if you are to become a truly successful leader. The primary tension in life, which really prevents us from being total in energy, thought, and action is this oscillation and constant change of inner mood. The whole secret is to relax with this rise and fall of the wave that is life. If you can learn to ride the wave well, nothing seems negative anymore. And you also come to know that the positive never lasts for eternity. You are prepared for both. This level of preparedness is really the secret of being able to ascend to a higher truth. To achieve your highest heights.

The seed of the highest is within us, but it is a very small possibility for it to truly germinate and sprout into a flower and fruit-bearing tree. It must be prepared to go through all sorts of climates, all sorts of weather conditions, only then can it truly blossom. And that is what the essence of leadership is. To make things come to a fruition, to create value. This requires courage. This requires being able to throw oneself into the situation, whatever it is. Whether it seems positive or not. Not to panic. Most people panic when it comes to facing negative situations or rather what they perceive to be negative situations. But that is exactly what differentiates the great leader from the mediocre one. The great leader is not like the mediocre one in the sense that he is not in a state of panic, of fear. And hence does not drown in the water even when the wave is unsuitable. He can ride the wave more easily because he is at one with it. He is not struggling against it. He is going with it. He is flowing with it, and this state of flow, this inward state of psychological and spiritual flow is essentially the secret of being total. Otherwise, everything seems like a disturbance.

Life is so dynamic in nature that one keeps going from one circumstance to the other. Constant change is happening but if you accept change as the order of life, it will create a new vitality within yourself. And this vitality will be transferred to those you lead. People keep choosing between pleasure and pain, but the person of true spirituality knows that between these two extremes of pleasure and pain is the balanced state of peaceful inner being. This total state of inner peace is an attitude where one is not escaping from anything, but confronting whatever life offers. One goes beyond both happiness and unhappiness. Only then does one attain this state of bliss, of joy. If only we can look beyond immediate circumstances and stop getting distracted by them, do we attain such totality. This is the secret of all great heroes of mythology. Their ability to transcend ordinary situations and keep moving toward a higher joy, a higher place.

Be trusting and be free to put your whole energy into what you do. Do not hold anything back. Within you is infinite energy, inexhaustible. It is simply a question of accepting circumstances, of accepting challenges. It is what you want to be which determines things, not circumstances. The potential is within you. It just requires that you bring your total self into it.

CHAPTER-17

Karma Yoga

LESSON: The spiritual philosophy of Karma Yoga implies working without being bound by limits or fears. It means surrendering one's ego during all thoughts and actions, and thereby becoming bold and dynamic in all one does! It is a crucial principle for leaders—and for all those seeking true success—to understand. It frees the mind, making one go beyond pettiness, expectations, and boundaries. Karma Yoga is the greatest key for expanding one's life and leadership spectrum.

The secret of Karma Yoga is to change one's vision from looking towards the outside to looking at the inner being. In the midst of work, most people are concerned with the outside, the exterior world. Hardly anybody emphasizes that the ideal leader, the karma yogi, is one who understands that the subtle is more important than the gross. In other words, the stream of consciousness gives birth to material events.

It is our internal attitude which is the determining factor in any work. In leadership positions, by knowing this simple principle one becomes relaxed even in the midst of the most difficult problem. Because you understand that the outer results are not the real thing you need to concentrate on. So it immediately takes away the sense of anxiety for results, and the work spontaneously moves towards real fruition—because now the work is invested with your concentrated and undisturbed energy! You are cool within, and out of that coolness is born a real dynamism of action. So from the point of view of karma yoga, we must unlearn this whole obsession with material things and material results. Focus on having insight into your inner being. That is what makes you truly alive, that is what keeps every action of yours fresh.

The source of where you are acting from is deep within you, and it is higher than the material sphere. It is the space from which your wisdom comes. It is your inner nature. Through this understanding, you can work without self-consciousness and anxiety. So doing, you gather real courage to jump into the deep end. You become afraid of nothing, because nothing can make you afraid anymore. Success or failure is simply a by-product of that which you are doing, but now it has become more affirmative, more pure, because you are flowing into that which you are doing. You are not becoming frozen or stuck by the thought of the results. So it's a very positive attitude with which to approach leadership.

A lot of work related and leadership related issues are centred around negativity simply because peoples' egos come in between. Where there is ego there is bound to be negativity. Real freedom comes from being so inwardly free that you feel like a pure energy, acting out of the totality of your life spirit. All the parts of your being come together without any mental barrier. So you can do your work with great joy. And this joy itself is extremely infectious—it creates a vibe within yourself, and within others. You begin acting out of a deeper space—that which has been called the void, the *shunya*. Your defensive armour has been dropped, because you no longer feel that anything can hurt you.

You see, the problem with people is that they wear a defence around themselves. So that failures cannot hurt them. But the karma yogi accepts vulnerability in such a manner, that the quality of action is transformed. So the emphasis is not on the action itself, but the quality of it. Most people's energy never reaches the threshold of freedom in action, because they are almost as if enclosed by the fear of results. Hence they cannot really make great things happen. Yet each person is capable of tremendous energy that is life-transforming and circumstance-transforming. The only thing needed is to be overflowing with ecstatic and tireless exuberance. Yet that never happens if we worry about being able to find the path ahead wondering whether we will stumble and fall.

The real understanding for the karma yogi, as Krishna says in the Bhagavad Gita, is that the guide exists within us all. All you have to do is allow that guide to surface, and spontaneously act through you. The inner guide is what matters. It is the most important part of you. It is what takes you from feeling very limited, to feeling like your very heart is involved in your work, with bliss and creativity. There is eventually no good action or creative action which is born out of misery. Creative action comes out of spiritual fullness. The power to sing your song in life with an intensity that takes you to the highest peak of your own consciousness. All strength and courage in life derives out of the way your inner being is allowed to express itself.

So Karma Yoga is the situation where the inner being, the hidden guide, within us, is allowed to unstintingly enjoy the very process and journey that it has been placed in within the material world. From the point of view of the leader, the achiever, this implies that we are not to put our hopes upon particular things happening, but truly live the moments we have as beautifully and powerfully as possible. The problem with the thought mechanism is that it often breeds jealousy, ego, comparisons of all sorts. Hence we must have the ability to look beyond such thoughts, and to look at that pure space which is not just result-oriented but is consciousness-oriented. Results are only a by-product that follow.

Enjoy the journey, and the destination will be reached effortlessly! Not only quickly, but also in a state of joy. And that is the quality we must seek to imbibe as leaders within the world. Karma Yoga means that more efforts have to be made to do your work with greater consciousness. The determining factor is how far we have been attentive to our inner being, how devoted we have been to our inner awareness of greater possibilities.

It has been observed throughout human history that truly great people have a certain grace in the way they act. Their efficiency is born out of deep enjoyment of their work. They do not look at circumstances as something to be endured, but rather have the ability to meet the circumstances very smilingly. As if nothing can touch them. They are in a state that they do not respond to the ego, but through the relaxed spaces of inner vision. Some of the most successful innovators have been those who have not relied on being calculating or clever, but instead have functioned very spontaneously and effortlessly. Even in a state of great effort, they have the ability to be cool, to be detached. And this is what allows them to do what others have not been able to do, because the real stamp of individuality at work and in leadership is when the individuality of your inner nature is allowed to function with utmost freedom. You function from the innermost part of yourself, and the results surface as if spontaneously. This is Karma Yoga.

CHAPTER-18

The Generous or 'Danveer' Leader

LESSON: Generosity expands you, miserliness contracts you. Be a 'giving' leader! Share your energy freely, and it will resound back to you a thousandfold. Great leadership is ultimately about motivating yourself and others through the power of sharing whatever abilities life has bestowed you with.

The generous or *danveer* leader enjoys a different level of trust than others. In Indian mythology, it is the great hero Karna who is known to be actually generous in thoughts and actions. And even though eventually the story of the Mahabharat talks about his tragic end, it is doubtless that he towers over all the other Pandavs in legend, mainly because of this one quality of his. Even today, people consider him to be a true hero despite his several faults.

The point is, if you wish to leave a really enduring legacy as a leader, you must be generous. Generosity is not distribution of material goods. It is essentially sharing of good energy that uplifts others. You should not be taken advantage of—people should be able to respect your generosity, willing to take risks for you and for what you represent as a leader.

There's an old Indian story which has been repeated in the West. It is about the shepherd who loses his sheep, but who has such generosity of heart that he leaves all the other sheep and searches for that one lost sheep. And finding it, he brings it home happily. There might not have been any practical need for him to do so, but his generosity of heart sends a message to others, as well as fulfils his own role as a 'leader' or guardian of the pack. The idea is this: real meaning in our lives shines through in our smallest gestures of generosity, of heart! Heartfelt gestures make the quality of life and leadership meaningful. There is absolutely no meaning without generosity of heart. And generosity means to create an aura of warmth around yourself. That does not mean being weak. It simply implies reaching out to people and making them believe that you care. It creates respect.

Ultimately, the vibration between people is the

most important thing when it comes to a team. And the vibration cannot come of some 'hierarchy'. In the realm of feelings, nobody is higher or lower. A good leader remembers that. So the ability to transform the consciousness of people is not about the knowledge we share, but about the simple clarity that together you can achieve victory. That together you can be a force that will not fail. And this tone is set by the way a leader can make his team believe in his own generosity of spirit.

Through the ages, great leaders have been able to transfer the generosity of energy onto their teams. It is best exemplified in the battlefield, and through the mythology and history of the world. Alexander could make his troops believe that he is for them, and he is ready to give his all for them. That is generosity of spirit, and that inspires like nothing else can. Generosity allows people to gather courage about their own selves, and therefore deliver better and better results. It also allows the leader himself to feel more vitally alive and valuable. One's way of functioning, one's aura and appeal itself changes, because one is in a state of flow with one's team, and this opens up a present-moment dynamism of energy within others.

C H A P T E R - 1 9

Leela:
The Art of Playfulness

LESSON: We realize the unlimited energies of ourselves through being playful in consciousness. This is important for leaders at all levels: it enables one to face even the toughest situations with clarity, speed, exuberance, patience, inspiration, and wisdom. It helps create excellence at decision-making, allows us to think laterally and 'out of the box', and inspires others through its effortlessness. Playfulness removes all psychological blocks and fears. It is a reflection of the divine quality within us.

Become more playful in your life and leadership style. The greatest leaders throughout history have often been playful. For example, Abraham Lincoln, even in the midst of all his serious decision-making, was known to have a rather delightful streak in him. He used to love to entertain people with stories and anecdotes. Also in the realm of politics, Nelson Mandela was known to be very often delightful in his leadership style, instead of being over-aggressive.

In the spiritual philosophy of Hinduism the concept of *leela* is very important. The avatar Krishna has been said to be in the state of leela, of playfulness, in all he did. And this concept is a very liberating force. It frees up one's style. Ultimately, the real leader has to be unconditional in his approach of serving people. Out of this sense of service—without expectations, in his state of deep self-delight—an energy is created within the work he does. In existence everything is interrelated. Nobody exists as an island. And a leader is somebody who constantly links people and things together. The quality of playfulness joins people, interconnects people. This is what Hindu philosophy believes in. Out of the state of playfulness, the true quality of your nature is allowed to reach higher potential. Each person is only a small drop in the ocean of existence, but through the aspect of playfulness becomes joined to the infinite ocean of truth. If only our leaders have a greater sense of humanity, delighting in peace and brotherhood, a new age in human happiness can arise.

Much of the faults in human society arise because leaders think they have to instigate people to negative things in order to lead them. It's very sad that a lot of leaders destroy the capacity of people to be affectionate to one another or to work as a cohesive team. But a truly positive leader instils the ideal of good warriorhood, that ideal being playful co-operation. In this lies the great secret of bonding within teams.

It is almost like children playing a game and forming their own teams. And they gel very nicely for the task at hand, which might be for a particular game. But the idea is because they come together in a state of pure playfulness, they're able to create team bonding much faster than adults normally can. So a playful attitude is really important, because through it people become immersed in what they do. And through it they access the vastness of consciousness, creating positive consciousness within the group. Let this quality of playfulness spread over your life, and you will realize that it rejuvenates you. It creates a cycle of happiness, a circle of peace, of silence, of enjoyment within yourself. And this is really what you should be aiming at as a leader.

If you yourself find a good state of being, the work you do automatically has a great harmony, a great order, and you're able to join things together, thereby creating something new.

Playfulness implies breaking borders, dropping resistance, cooperating; and all these things are very essential to a leader for him or her to inspire people. It is never enough to inspire teams through mental ideas alone. It is also important to appeal to their inner depths, and nothing appeals more to the inner depth of people than the idea of carrying out their activities in a state of joy, in a state of play. That is when one becomes transformed from the ordinary to the excellent.

Essentially, God himself is defined in old Indian philosophy as being the ultimate player, who creates and destroys this universe as part of His cosmic play. And we are only actors in that play, who can choose to play a part with the spirit of delight. That is the spiritual attitude. Of course, we must be determined to persevere and be hard-working, but at the same time we are not to take ourselves too seriously or our roles too seriously.

Every position of power is temporary. It is your state of being which matters. Whether you lose that power tomorrow or not, you can retain that sense of playfulness within you. It means you are a real success if you can do so. That is what real fulfilment is all about. It is a noble vision of functioning, beyond logic and calculation. Man has become too calculating, which is why he is sometimes not creative and dynamic enough. This very fact of calculating the results of things sometimes becomes the hindrance, becomes the limitation of a leader. Because he does not open up, but creates walls around himself. Sadly, many leaders of today function in a very negative manner. They want to wall out people from each other. They want to isolate ideas and people. The truly great leader is one who liberates ideas and people, and does it with blissful, playful consciousness. Through this very dispersal of ideas comes about great transformation.

Playfulness is a state of inner coolness. It is a process of transforming our inner energies into cool and dynamic flow. And when we are flowing with all our energy combined, integrated within, in a joyful manner, all the obstacles in our path get washed away.

Mankind is faced with so many crises of so many different sorts—whether these are environmental, political, religious, national and international, and so on. We are on the verge of self-destruction, and a lot of this has to do with simply bad leadership. The whole paradigm of leadership has to shift and evolve into making leaders themselves more firmly rooted in an attitude of cooperative consciousness. Authentic leadership needs compassion and consciousness more than ever. Leadership needs a sense of individual-centring, a sense that a person's best consciousness flows into the collective consciousness of civilization. That is essentially what a leader should be focusing on. To uplift the collective consciousness and not debase it. Hence the entire emphasis and the importance of the spiritual aspect when it comes to leadership and success.

The quest for thousands of years in India was to create evolved individuals, yet so much of that thought has been missing for too long. It is time for it to be given adequate attention, and to bring the consciousness of a playful and joyful attitude towards work more and more, in order to evolve great leaders.

Parallelism of the Material and Spiritual

LESSON: The foundation for successful life and leadership is bringing a balance between the material and spiritual aspects. This happens through the power of consciousness: our consciousness determines our state of being. Hence, even while dealing with worldly things and responsibilities, remember to manifest the core spiritual qualities within your consciousness: truth, harmony, peacefulness, calm, non-anxiousness. This makes your work rich from the very source. It is the secret of success, fulfilment, contentment, and true higher achievement.

The ancient Hindu view was that the truly successful person is she or he who can have both external and internal achievements, in a smooth parallelism. That is to say, the external things (power, position, wealth, and fame) always need to run parallel to achievements in the internal sphere (these being a joyful mind, peace, calmness, affection, and a universal view of existence).

If external material achievements do not move in a smooth parallelism with internal spiritual values, they're absolutely meaningless. And if internal achievements do not move in a smooth parallelism with external achievements, they do not come within the sphere of material leadership: they are good and important in their own way, but not necessarily for influencers in the material realm.

Maturity in leadership is about integrating both aspects. Now, the ego can project that the material does not need the spiritual and the deeply psychological aspects of being to evolve. But the fact of the matter is that real revolution in leadership attitudes begins with the revolution in human consciousness. It is essentially about being able to radiate certain values. The beginning is always internal, and gradually it starts manifesting as the external. Essentially, a leader has to see that what he seeks internally will radiate and shine through in external achievements. Eventually culminating in a smooth parallelism.

The problem with human beings is that the more materially successful they become, the more becomes the forgetfulness of their internal sphere. But we stop progressing on the journey of life without evolving eternally. So the track of the internal should not be sacrificed at the altar of the material. This simply means we should not be losing our originality, not forgetting who we really are and settling for a pale reflection of ourselves (as achievers of the purely material).

Man has to understand that without the evolution of consciousness, life is almost meaningless. If the essential is missing, then all is missing. So the correction has to be made in leadership philosophy, and the correction is simply that we do not miss the completeness of victory—that of our consciousness. The evolution of consciousness is the greatest success of life. It is the culmination of what life is in its totality. The catalyst must be internal.

Remember, there is always a relationship between what is inner and what is outer. There cannot be an effect without a cause, and the cause always lies in the subtle portion of existence. That is what spirituality is based on. The cause always lies almost hidden, and when it comes to human beings that hidden part is within the deepest recesses of our consciousness. When the provocation of the inner is positive, its fruition in the material world is also positive. When the provocation of the inner is negative, its fruition in the material world is also negative. The truth about humanity is that no matter who or where, all are searching for the spiritual aspect of life! That is the most basic search of man: the search for spiritual satisfaction. It is as important as the search for material fulfilment, if not more so. Of course the basic needs of life have to be met, but beyond that there must come about a parallel evolution of both aspects. The sources of joy and the sources of fulfilment are within us. The material part of ourselves is actually the superficial part—it can bring about a certain happiness in life, but that is a very transitory and passing experience. Lasting joy and lasting fulfilment only happen at the deepest core of ourselves. So we have to pay attention more and more to the more sublime, more beautiful part of ourselves—that is the inner being of ourselves. Bring that to an optimum state. That way, we automatically and spontaneously become far more radiant and charismatic as leaders, and as role models of any sort. Good things elicit good responses, and that is essentially what an able leader does: get heartfelt, co-operative responses from people so that together they can move on to something that is larger than the individuals.

The spiritual golden rule is: The external is always rejuvenated through the action of the internal. The light source is internal. The heart of creation itself is in a hidden internal truth. What we see within the world is only the effect of that truth. So be more in touch with your internal self, and you will see yourself acting more positively in the world. Spirituality is essentially the pair of wings which allows the human being to go higher into the open sky of truth and fulfilment. The funny part is, that the more successful some people become, the more and more lost they often become: lost often in things that are not really essential. They start believing that it is alright to sacrifice, substitute, or forget the inner sources of existence. But this forgetfulness is the real problem. The most evolved leader is he or she who has deep insight into reality. With such insight comes an understanding of that which is holistic, beneficial for the planet and for fellow human beings. Eventually, a leader in his or her own way is to become a positive contributor to this planet that we exist upon.

It is really interesting in today's age that science has been coming to a parallelism with ancient spirituality, especially in the realm of consciousness. There have been huge advancements in neuroscience, which is validating that which the old religions held to be true. The human mind is a channel for deep consciousness, and is naturally a determinant for its own fulfilment. Contentment, in other words, is not dependent upon the happenings of the outer, but can in fact be the creator of them.

So the human spirit is the starting point. The really relevant thing in life is to attain an understanding of this human spirit within us, this immense depth of our own mind and being. This aspect of cause and effect of internal and external states is not limited to the human being alone, it also exists in the natural world. For example, music has been shown to affect the growth of plants. Something as subtle as music can affect the way plants grow. Experiments have been conducted about how the very vibration of certain kinds of classical music can create a positive energy for plants to bear fruit and flowers to a greater degree. If music can do that to plants, what can your own inner music—the music of the human spirit—do to determine the blossoming of your own potential! Realize your own unlimited energy sources, your inner potential. And then only do you move towards fulfilling and creating material joy, and achieving your fullest material potential.

Vedas, Upanishads, and Sri Ram for Leaders

LESSON: Hinduism views our fundamental nature as a reflection of the highest Supreme Reality. Within every cell of our being vibrates the Highest: this is a core message of Hinduism, at the very heart of Upanishadic and Vedic wisdom. Understanding this expands your vision of 'self', making you act with far greater release of your highest potential. It is crucial for leaders to have a holistic vision of themselves and their true spiritual nature. Know that you are a pure soul, a purely spiritual being at your very essence! This makes you tremendously fearless, awake, blissful, thereby awakening the full power of latent and unique energy you have been bestowed with. And this energy is utilized within your life and leadership roles for the welfare of all.

The Vedas and the Upanishads give us some of the most wonderful lessons when it comes to the consciousness required for dynamic leadership. The Brihadaranyaka Upanishad in the Yajur Veda says, '*Aham Brahmasmi*' meaning that 'I am the absolute, I am Brahman, I am the ultimate truth!' And the Maitrayaniya Upanishad, also from the Yajur Veda, says: 'Where there is joy, there is creation; where there is no joy, there is no creation. Know the nature of joy!' So we can see that the Vedas and Upanishads are emphasizing a few things very much—that within you is the absolute truth, within you is the highest consciousness, and within you is the highest capacity for joy. If your consciousness is full of this confidence, zest for life, and deep belief in self, nothing can stop you from being a very dynamic person in life. And that is the very secret of great leadership: begin with your consciousness. Therein resides the seed of how your life and leadership success turns out to be.

You are not distant from the celestial, the supreme, the all-powerful, the divine. You are a microcosm and a part and parcel of it. Your consciousness is a reflection of the divine; feel that! And when you feel that, you feel a completeness of energy, you feel psychologically liberated of all limitations. And great leaders have this fundamental quality: they are psychologically free of feeling limited, feeling small, and so on. They have great self-confidence! So the Vedas and Upanishads of India give you the ultimate self-confidence, telling you that it is simply up to you. Realize yourself as part of the infinite, and then you feel whole within yourself, you feel dynamic within yourself. You feel yourself empowered in mind, body, and soul. And so doing, not only do you come to self-understanding, but you come to a great dynamism of passion in your role as a leader. That is the very secret of inspiring yourself and inspiring others.

You see, it is very important for a leader to be able to transform their idea about themselves. And that is what the Upanishads and the Vedas are doing! They make you feel the true treasure of yourself within you, the true power of your self-potential. And when you feel the power of your self-potential, not only do you become more confident in your own being, but you are able to inspire true confidence in others, because you 'walk the talk' by first believing in yourself. And that spontaneously takes you towards a higher and higher fulfilment in whatever leadership role you have. This is the intuitively conscious way to become more powerful in mind and spirit. It is the very key not only to a more meditative life, but to a more materially successful life also; because your individuality shines through when you realize yourself as the highest consciousness and highest joy at the same time! First know that you are capable of the highest possibilities;

then you are able to radically transform the environment around you.

Everything begins with self-belief. And that is what the Vedic texts do: they instil us with a great self-belief, taking us to a truer confidence than that which is conditioned in us through society. It is all about the greater consciousness of your soul-essence. And when your confidence is born out of your essential soul-essence or soul-consciousness, then you become intuitively and creatively powerful. You are able to not only live a life of greater wisdom, but a life where you spontaneously are able to carry the responsibility of leadership and manifest that more and more into your life. It is the very key of both higher realization and fulfilment.

As discussed previously, Sri Ram is taken to be the epitome of good leadership in Indian mythology. He demonstrates great leadership in his own life; but at the same time, is able to eloquently expound his spirituality-based leadership lessons for others. Sri Ram says: 'The inner soul—the atma within you—is completely blissful. Why must you think that sorrow exists in the soul? Thinking so is ignorance. Through true knowledge, this ignorance disappears!'

So Ram really teaches that we are to realize ourselves as sheer delightful bliss at the level of the soul. This is the highest spiritual teaching of ancient India. It says that the root consciousness of yourself is pure bliss. And when you realize yourself to be pure bliss at your root consciousness, a great confidence is born in you; a great self-belief is born in you. You are able to tide by any circumstances in your life with a great passion of energy. And that is the hallmark of great leaders! You see, the difference between excellent leaders and mediocre ones is the fundamental energy that they carry. There are some leaders who don't realize the infinity of their potential and therefore they cannot inspire others to find their own potential realization. A great leader is one who moves towards his or her own potential realization and catalyzes that process in others too. But it all begins with realizing the very essence of yourself. And the very essence of yourself, says Ram, is that you are part of the great blissfulness that is all of existence, that is all of the cosmos. You are a wave in the great ocean of bliss! Know yourself as part of the bliss. And all of creation is blissful. That is the fundamental component of creation. This is a great teaching of Sanatan Dharma or Hinduism, but is also really the root of all mystical consciousness. The ability to know yourself capable of as much bliss as the highest seer, Rishi, sage, or Buddha—this is the element of not only spiritual realization or *Samadhi* as it's called in the Hindu philosophy, but is also the very root of transcending all your sense of limitations, all your fear of circumstances. And when you do that, you start living with your innermost energy; and your innermost energy is able to spread throughout your activities in whatever you do, in whoever you relate with and so on and so forth. It vibrates within you!

All great leaders who have inner charisma have this sense of delight within their being! They know that at the very soul there is nothing which can stop them because they are comprised of bliss. And that no matter how circumstances seem, no matter how big a crisis may seem, they can overcome, because they are able to tap into an inner strength, an inner power of possibility-consciousness and bliss-consciousness. The very fact of knowing oneself as comprised of bliss or Ananda as it's called in Sanskrit, makes one feel that one is part of the highest. In Hinduism, the *Paramatman* or the supreme being, and the *Jivatma* or the individual being are really part and parcel of the same reality. In fact, the Upanishads say, '*Tat Tvam Asi.*' And Sri Ram says: 'Understand the sameness of the Paramatman, the supreme being, and Jivatman, the living being. Firstly, you must realize the meaning of the Upanishadic statement, Tat Tvam Asi. Tat implies Paramatman, Tvam implies Jivatman, and Asi means are. Hence, it implies that the Paramatman and Jivatman are one and the same! Don't attempt to differentiate them, nor seek separate attributes in them.'

What Sri Ram is saying is that the highest possibility of the supreme soul is also possible to the individual soul. In other words, never think of yourself as less than the absolute reality. Remember that you are part of the great universal energy. Remember that you are a child of this wondrous cosmos! And so doing, empower yourself from within. In the Upanishads, the boy Svetaketu receives these same words from the guru—Tat Tvam Asi, meaning that you are the highest!

When you understand this, a great revolution happens in your mind and heart. You realize that you are not ordinary. Each of us is extraordinary. Each of us has a great, extraordinary ability to manifest the divine energy through our thoughts and actions in life! And the great leader is one who undertakes to channel this energy through his or her actions. So doing, she or he becomes not only a good example for others to follow but is able to fulfil herself or himself through this life. You see, Hindu philosophy says that the microcosm and the macrocosm are fundamentally the same; and so does quantum physics! Quantum physics says that the smallest particles are actually behaving just as the largest phenomena in the universe behave. So at the atomic and the subatomic level, things are as they are at the galactic level, at the interstellar level, and at the universal scale of things. So it implies that if you magnify yourself in consciousness, you will see that you are fundamentally very much like the great universal energy. And feeling that within yourself, a great strength comes to you; you no longer feel weak! You feel that the highest awareness, the highest courage is all available to you! And these are the qualities which a great leader needs.

A great leader needs to have a very high degree of courage and a great degree of awareness. These are the fundamental consciousness qualities. Know that the smallest entity and the largest entity share a commonality. It is like if you magnify a part of a leaf with an electron microscope infinitely, go into an infinite regress into the smaller components, you find that there is a never-ending process of duplication, even at the physical level. So also at the level of soul, we are connected to the super-soul, what we may call God and so on. Understanding this, your energy explodes within yourself. You find a great vigour in your being, a great strength. Finding strength within yourself is at the heart of great leadership ability. And at the very heart of Sanatan Dharma, the Hindu wisdom—what we may call Sankhya, Vedanta and so on—is this truth.

Sri Ram is known to the world as being the hero of the Ramayan, the great epic of India. But people forget that he's also the hero of the Yoga Vasishtha Maharamayan, which is the greatest—and world's lengthiest—discourse on spirituality. Vasishtha and Ram talk about the inner glory, the inner world of ours which is so full of power, so full of strength, so full of splendour, so full of divine ability. And so doing, they take us towards understanding our essential, delightful energy within ourselves—which is unlimited. Seeing yourself as unlimited, you realize that you are indeed part of the highest reality, the highest energy: Tat Tvam Asi! Through this comes an extraordinary explosion of strength within you, an extraordinary confidence within you.

We become under-confident because we don't identify ourselves with the higher reality. We somehow feel psychologically less than what we should be feeling. Our thoughts somehow make us anxious. The inner glory of ourselves goes missing. And a great leader is one who never forgets the inner glory of the soul, the inner glory of human consciousness. If, within your consciousness, you feel a great deal of inner glory, if you understand the treasure of consciousness within yourself, then you become unstoppable because you feel full of inner confidence, psychological confidence, spiritual confidence, and so on. You feel like you're multidimensional. You leave your inhibitions behind. Good leadership requires us to leave our inhibitions behind. You see, a corollary in

Indian mythology is that of Arjun on the battlefield of Kurukshetra, facing his cousins in battle. And the whole secret of that episode which has been immortalized in the epic Mahabharat, and more specifically in the Bhagavad Gita, is the process of Lord Krishna demystifying this sense of paralysis and mental anxiousness that Arjun has fallen into.

Arjun has fallen into anxiety, has fallen into restlessness. He has forgotten his identity with the greater reality. He has forgotten that within himself exists a great kingdom of the divine, a hidden kingdom; it is for him to discover once again in his own interior being! And once he realizes that he himself is part of the divine, he feels more conscious, he feels more aware; he realizes his responsibility as a leader of men, as a setter of an example to other warriors on the battlefield. And finding this essential soul-consciousness, he is able to go into battle as a warrior with a *completeness* of self.

Now again, Sri Ram constantly teaches the consciousness that we reflect the largest. For example, he tells Hanuman who's his greatest devotee: 'It is the Divine (the Paramatman) that you see reflected in all living beings (the Jivatman). It is like the vast sky being reflected in every river, lake, or pond. The Divine is like the vast sky whose reflections keep changing! All living beings reflect the Divine.'

So we can see Ram repeating this sameness of the Jivatman and the Paramatman, the individual soul and the super-soul or God; this identity of one with the other. To understand his words, we need a great deal of openness. We need to understand that concept of quantum physics which says that essentially we are comprised of the same cosmic components, the same stardust, so to speak. It could be a blade of grass or it could be a tall oak tree; all are essentially comprised of the same material factor at the subatomic level. The smallest is reflective of the largest. And this is the whole attitude of the Sanatan Dharma, this is the whole attitude of Hindu philosophy—that spiritually, we are to a very profound degree connected to the highest reality of the divine. We are, in fact, a reflection of the divine! The glory of universal power resides within us. When you realize this, then you come to an understanding that within yourself, you are extraordinary; within yourself, you can be blissful; within yourself, you can be immeasurable.

This is the very root of confidence when it comes to leadership. It creates a certain fearlessness of being. And to be a great leader requires the sense of fearlessness. It requires you to move beyond all ideas of fear, all ideas of ego; and move towards the state of cheerfulness, move towards a flow of passionate energy so that you can manifest all the possibilities that you are capable of.

Hence, we can see that Hinduism teaches key leadership values; in fact, golden leadership values—at a very fundamental level! It tells us that we are capable of moving to any heights on this profound adventure called life. We are capable of opening up to the highest spiritual and material possibilities in life. It is simply a question of attitude. Sri Ram says again, 'The soul or Atman is distinct and different from all your other aspects: body, senses, mind, *prana* (vital energy). The soul is supremely blissful, absolute, non-dual, timeless and permanent, without form, without sin, and completely pure. When you realize this, you are liberated that very moment!'

So Ram again is emphasizing the inner richness of our individual worlds, that world which exists within us in our mind. We are infinitely rich. We are infinitely full of inner treasure! Realize this inner treasure. And so doing, you'll realize that you are full of courage, you are full of fearlessness, you are full of an inner wisdom. In the end, a good leader needs a great deal of inner wisdom. But Ram is saying that you already have wisdom within you. It's simply a question of recognizing it, of realizing it. It is a question of perception of your own innate reality. Realize that the whole energy-field that we call the cosmos is in fact a product of the same soulful consciousness that resides within us! In the Upanishads, it's described as the ultimate nothingness, that which resides within all things. In a key Upanishadic lesson, the Guru tells the disciple to take the seed of the Nyagrodh tree, and to keep breaking it till he comes to realize that at the essence and end there is only a 'nothingness' within the seed! Yet it can give birth to a tree! The learning is this: out of nothingness comes everything. So there is an essential nothingness; that which we may call soulful energy, soulful consciousness. Out of that, we all come! Hence identify with soul energy and soul consciousness alone, not with material events or objects! This is what the boy-sage (rishi) Ashtavakra tells the mighty King Janak in the Ashtavakra Gita! Janak is considered a supreme leader (in fact mentioned by Krishna too in the Bhagavad Gita) but even he has to learn this lesson: that more important than material events and material things are the soul energy and soul consciousness behind them! That is the basis of spiritually inspired leadership, and it helps take Janak toward enlightened living as an individual and as a leader of people.

The great leader is one who's able to catalyze his consciousness into realizing its own richness; who's able to live a dynamic life by knowing that he is not limited to mind and not limited to body. But rather, belongs to this great wealth of consciousness from which everything comes. Very interestingly, Sri Ram also says: 'Via the process of *Neti Neti* or "not this not this" (the process of negation or mental elimination), you must endeavour to realize the true nature of the soul, the Atma! The world consists of both good and evil, and we must investigate it in essence. Always take the essence and get rid of the rest, just as you'd throw away the mango seed after enjoying the mango's delicious taste. Know this: the soul is deathless—having no childhood, youth, or old age.'

Ram is emphasizing something very intrinsic to the Vedic vision. He says: eliminate all that is non-essential, and instead simply take the essence. Don't get into trivial pursuits. Leaders at all levels need to have this clarity which Ram is talking about: leave that which is unnecessary. Take the juice of the mango; you can throw away the seed. Chip away at falsehood, and the truth shall be found! You have to do nothing at all but discard the non-essential. So this very concept of Neti Neti is a process of cleansing. It is basically a process of saying that the leader, the individual, should not be so concerned about the trivial. All that we need to do is to recognize the trivial for what it is! Don't get shaken by circumstances. Realize the intrinsic part of truth. And then you are able to become a person of discernment, wisdom, strength.

This is also a technique which Gautam Buddha used to prescribe a lot. The whole essence of it is being minimalistic. Of looking at the core of truth, of distilling the essence, and discarding all other things as those can be distracting! Get rid of the surrounding untruth. This minimalism is what Steve Jobs, co-founder of Apple, used to believe in. He used to believe in this process of Neti Neti or elimination. He was famous for going into retreats with his people and while taking their ideas for Apple products, he used to simply throw most of those ideas out. He used to just choose very, very few; he used to say that the rest doesn't matter. And that the focus is to be on the essential. Not on the excess baggage.

And that is what dynamism in leadership needs: the ability to get rid of excess baggage, the ability to get rid of notions of anxious thought, the ability to look at core truth, to get to the crux of the matter. This is also the very basis of the Zen Buddhism of Japan. Hence, be minimalistic in your leadership attitude. Throw away the baggage and be light in your leadership vision. Don't get engrossed in too many concepts, don't get engrossed in too many conditioned ways of functioning. Good leaders function with a great deal of inner clarity and inner wisdom. That requires a freedom from conditioned notions. The whole idea of disruptive thinking in today's world stems from this idea that we can get rid of whatever has been taken to be absolute truth in the past. Discard that which is non-essential, chip away at untruth, and fulfil your life and role as a leader with your own extraordinary revolutionary vision.

Hindu wisdom is essentially about inculcating freshness of vision. And for good leadership today, freshness of vision is key. Newness, innovative consciousness, and path-breaking thought requires an elimination of conditioned concepts. And elimination of conditioned concepts is what Upanishadic/Vedic knowledge is at its heart. It teaches spirituality-based lessons of enabling the new, the fresh, with clarity of consciousness. And readiness to move into the new, with clarity of consciousness, is the new paradigm of great leaders. Find the new, find great new energy and fresh ideas: through that you'll find your inner power, the power of heart and soul! Ultimately, being a leader of clarity, a leader of minimalism, is also being a leader of empathy—because such an individual is able to find new ways to connect people to people, to connect products to people, and so on. Stick to the essential! And when you do that, you're able to explore the vastness of your own self-potential. You're able to find a great freedom and blissfulness in your own mind and heart; and at the same time, you're able to do things with far more energy and clarity.

Acknowledgements

I wish to express my humble gratitude to the people who have made this series possible:

Anuj Bahri, my super literary agent at Red Ink.

Shikha Sabharwal and Gaurav Sabharwal, my wonderful publishers at Fingerprint! Publishing and their team.

Garima Shukla, my amazing and brilliant editor.

Family—my parents, partner Sohini, sister Priti, nieces, nephews, et al: you are my rock.

Gratitude also to my support team, friends, mentors, and well-wishers over the years.

Pranay is a mystic philosopher. He is an expert on Indian and world spirituality.

Pranay's modules on 'Advanced Spirituality for Leadership and Success' (PowerTalks/MysticTalks for public and corporate audiences) have won global acclaim.

Pranay is also a theatre personality and playwright. His original productions such as *From Kabir to Kavi* and *Soul Stir* have been acclaimed by world luminaries for their path-breaking spiritual content.

Pranay and his partner Sohini run the socio-cultural philanthropic commune TAS, whose initiatives such as 'Theatre Against Drugs' (for addicts), 'Geetimalya' (for underprivileged children) and 'Shohaag' (for women empowerment) are well-known and have become movements.

Presently, Pranay is collating his discourses on mind-body-spirit themes for various book series.

Connect with him on his website: pranay.org